THE ENVIRONMENT AND THE HUMAN CONDITION

An interdisciplinary series edited by faculty
at the University of Illinois

GREEN NATURE/HUMAN NATURE

Green Nature/Human Nature

❧

THE MEANING OF PLANTS
IN OUR LIVES

❧

Charles A. Lewis

UNIVERSITY OF ILLINOIS PRESS
URBANA AND CHICAGO

First Illinois paperback, 1996
© 1996 by Charles A. Lewis

Manufactured in the United States of America

1 2 3 4 5 C P 5 4

This book is printed on acid-free paper.

Library of Congress Cataloging-in-Publication Data

Lewis, Charles A., 1924–
    Green nature/human nature : the meaning of plants in our lives /
Charles A. Lewis.
        p.   cm. — (The Environment and the human condition)
    Includes index.
    ISBN 0-252-02213-0 (cloth : alk. paper). — ISBN 0-252-06510-7
(pbk. : alk. paper)
    1. Human-plant relationships.   I. Title.   II. Series.
QK46.5.H85L48 1996
304.2'7—dc20   95-17506
                                                                    CIP

*T*o the gardening residents of the
New York City Housing Authority
who first opened my eyes to human
connections with green nature.

... while pursuing the humblest occupations—such as planting or cutting flowers, I had perceived, as a chink of light through a door opened quickly, a greater plan of things than our programme for the year, a larger world than that surrounding us, and one universal pattern of things, in which all existence has its place . . . I have felt peace descend on me while I have handled plants, so that a rhythm and harmony of being has been brought about. That harmony is the beginning of health. . . . There is a universal pattern, a pattern that flows like a stream, like the moving pattern of a dance. It is possible even through such contact with the earth as I have had, to be drawn into that pattern and move with it.

—Elaine Penwardin, *It's the Plants That Matter* (London: George Allen and Unwin, 1967)

Contents

Acknowledgments		xi
The Morton Arboretum		xv
Preface		xvii
1.	Green Nature	1
2.	Green Nature and Human Evolution	10
3.	Green Nature Observed	25
4.	Participation with Green Nature: Gardening	49
5.	Horticultural Therapy	74
6.	The Restorative Environment	106
7.	Toward a Green Tomorrow	121
	Conclusion	129
	Notes	135
	Index	143

Acknowledgments

This book represents what I have learned during thirty years of exploring people-plant relationships. As a horticulturist venturing into humanist concerns, I have been fortunate to have known many people who helped guide my steps, encouraged and supported my work, and were available to discuss concepts, theories, and the implications of their research.

Marion T. Hall, former director of the Morton Arboretum, permitted and encouraged my interest in human responses to nature throughout my twenty years of employment at the arboretum. He fostered broad thinking, allowing individuals to explore and grow in areas not directly related to their primary assignments. He also required a disciplined approach to my humanistic perspective on plants. Under Marion Hall, the Morton Arboretum granted me a three-year research fellowship, which allowed me to relinquish my duties as Collections Program administrator and initiate work on this book. Gerard T. Donnelly, who became director in 1990, allowed me to continue the research and writing that has resulted in this volume.

Patrick Horsbrugh, then a professor of architecture at Notre Dame University, was the first to point out to me the need to move beyond horticulture and introduced me to disciplines concerned with human responses to the environment.

Rachel Kaplan and Stephen Kaplan, pioneer environmental psychologists at the University of Michigan, have been mentors for my explorations since 1977. They emboldened me to think critically in this new area, exposed me to the literature, and shared their vitality and friendship. Their interest has been essential, and I am forever grateful.

Prentice and Virginia Bloedel of Bainbridge Island, Washington, intuitively understood the relationship between green nature and human nature and provided stimulation and funding for this work. I use the term *green nature* to identify not only the green entities that grow from the soil but also for all the associated processes—biological, physiological, and chemical—in plants, soil, and air that establish the living qualities of plant systems.

Roger Ulrich of Texas A&M University has been a consultant on environmental psychology, particularly psychophysiological responses. I appreciate his many suggestions and the wealth of research papers to which he led me.

Diane Relf, Virginia State University and Polytechnic Institute and chair of the People-Plant Council, is a horticulturist who early on understood the people-plant viewpoint. Her leadership in the field assures the continuity of research, networking, and distribution of information regarding human issues in horticulture. She also made valuable comments and suggestions on the book's preparation, as did Brian Orland of the Department of Landscape Architecture at the University of Illinois at Urbana-Champaign; Gordon Orians, professor of zoology at the University of Washington, Seattle; and Richard Mattson, professor of horticultural therapy at Kansas State University.

Mark Francis, chair of environmental design, University of California at Davis, helped with early stages of the manuscript and has been a continuing source of encouragement.

John Dwyer, director of the U.S. Forest Service North Central Forest Experiment Station, has been patron saint of this field, sponsoring research, calling conferences, and personally encouraging my efforts. At the Morton Arboretum, I have collaborated on research with Herbert Schroeder, a member of John Dwyer's staff.

Joan Lee Faust, former garden editor of the *New York Times*, encouraged publication of my first article, "Can You Grow Flowers on Avenue D?" in 1971 and has supported my work ever since, and Enid Haupt's 1972 grant to the American Horticultural Society funded my first empiric research into the human values of gardening.

I am grateful to the Walt Disney Corporation for granting permission to quote from an interview with Katy Moss Warner, director of parks horticulture at Walt Disney World, and to all of my people-plant colleagues who so generously shared their experiences for inclusion here.

And, finally, my wife, Sherry Rabbino, artist and editor extraordinary, has suffered through this manuscript with me for five years. She has been able to reform awkward sentences and pull together scattered thoughts. She has also spent endless hours at the computer making my thoughts readable. Without her support and expertise, I doubt that this volume would have appeared.

The Morton Arboretum

The Morton Arboretum, a botanical garden of trees, is located in the suburbs of Chicago, Illinois. Through research and education programs for the public and professionals, the Morton Arboretum advances understanding and appreciation of woody plants and the environment. Arboretum plant collections, gardens, and landscapes achieve scholarly museum purposes, and also provide the human values that this book celebrates.

Charles Lewis's thinking and this book developed during his twenty-year tenure at the Morton Arboretum as collections group administrator and later as a special research fellow dedicated to his writing. The Morton Arboretum is pleased to have supported Charles Lewis, the development of his ideas, and their expression in this book.

Preface

Why do gardeners find endless delight in the mysterious germination and growth of a seed? As if enchanted, we water, weed, dig, and dream. Why are our spirits so lifted by flowers, choosing them to mark the meaningful occasions of our lives, both happy and sad?

What compels many of us each fall to behave like lemmings, massing along roads and hiking trails to immerse ourselves in foliage aflame with color? And what draws us so powerfully to savor panoramic views? Highway engineers acknowledge this urge. Knowing we would stop anyway, they construct scenic overlooks where cars can pull off the road without drivers having to risk life and limb.

People and plants are entwined by threads that reach back to our very beginnings as a species. Woven tightly into the fabric of life, the threads are usually invisible unless one is snagged. Then, for a moment, its individual course can be traced, exposing a fragment of the complex pattern of our evolutionary development.

It seems we each harbor a hidden self that reacts without thinking to signals embedded within our bodies and in the outside world. Every subconscious response reveals threads that comprise the fabric of our lives, a protective cloak that has been woven about us for millennia to ensure our survival. Today, in a world largely shaped by intellect, those ancient intuitive threads are frequently pulled. We must learn to read them, for they provide insights into our basic humanity.

Our ties to the green world are often subtle and unexpected. It is not merely that hemoglobin and chlorophyll bear a striking similarity in structure, or that plants provide the pleasure of food and flowers. When people who garden find new friendships with neighbors, when a walk in the woods brings relief from pent-up tensions, or when a potted begonia restores vitality to a geriatric patient, we can begin to sense the power of these connections and their importance to physical and psychological well-being.

I was bonded with plants at an early age. As a small, curious boy, I once watched my grandmother crush a dried zinnia flower in her hand, then gently blow on the mixed pile of fragments. Petals and other chaff flew off, leaving tiny brown daggers on her palm. "Seeds to grow next year," she said. It seemed incredible that from these dead shards could bloom flowers for the coming summer. How did she know? Surely this was a kind of ancient wisdom, a secret my grandmother had learned in the old country and which she was now passing on to me. I was awed and excited by the chance to practice this magic, and, with her guidance, soon started my own tiny garden.

My family lived in Baltimore in a house with three upstairs bedrooms. To make additional sleeping space for their five children, my parents enclosed a portion of the downstairs porch with windows, which, because I was the eldest boy, became my bedroom. As an eight-year-old, feeling banished in that remote part of the house, I was terrorized each night by an assortment of imagined intruders threatening to enter my windowed room. Only when the sky began to brighten in the East would I finally relax and fall into a deep sleep.

Every morning, before climbing upstairs to rejoin the family, I would walk into the backyard in slippers and robe to visit my plants, noting any new leaves or buds that might have emerged overnight. They were my secret friends, "Charlie's babies," and I wanted reassurance that all was well with them. This early communion was deeply comforting, chasing away nocturnal fears and renewing my spirit at the beginning of each day. Only many years later did I realize how tightly the ritual had bonded my view of plants to my feelings about them.

This particular way of seeing made me aware of the benefits of people-plant interactions in a wide range of settings—hospitals, geriatric centers, drug rehabilitation institutions, and prisons. Such benefits are evidenced in the behavior of city-dwellers who seek relief from urban stress by frequenting parks or fleeing to weekend retreats in the country. Contact with green nature is essential to well-being and offers peace and assurance.

Why should this be true?

Since the 1960s I have been trying to discover answers to that question. This book explores what I have learned: As we garden, tramp through field or forest, stroll in city parks, or rest beneath a tree, we may come to an unexpected door that opens inward to self. What begins as recreation can lead to profound investigation of the questions of human existence.

There are deep reasons for our love affair with nature. We are creatures who evolved in an environment already green. Within our cells live memories of the role vegetation played in fostering our survival as a species. Plants reconnect that distant past, calling forth feelings of tranquility and harmony, restoring mental and physical health in a contemporary, technological world. Whether in pots, gardens, fields, or forests, living plants remind us of that ancient connection.

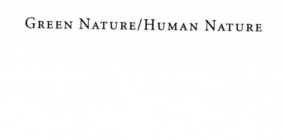

GREEN NATURE/HUMAN NATURE

1

Green Nature

Long before Homo sapiens first appeared, nature had cloaked the earth in a green mantle that nurtured all existing forms of life as well as those yet to be. The tattered remnants of that verdant covering are our inheritance. No longer continuous, it now exists only where we humans allow it to remain. Other pieces are usurped, deemed too valuable to be left "undeveloped," as civilization consumes them to feed its insatiable growth.

Yet green nature undauntingly adapts to the rhythms and conditions of each locale. The pervasive presence of vegetation ready to emerge wherever light, warmth, and moisture combine to create a potential habitat is visual evidence of the planet's irrepressible life force. Examples can be found in some of its least hospitable places.

In the Sonoran Desert, wildflowers seize the few precious spring rains to germinate, grow, bloom, and set seeds, completing their entire life-cycle in a matter of weeks. Annual ephemerals, they flourish with the same astonishing panache as a bouquet suddenly manifest in a magician's hand, and they vanish just as quickly. Visitors to the desert at other times of the year see no trace of this dazzling phenomenon.

Bristle-cone pines (*Pinus aristata*), the oldest living things on earth, are found in the White Mountains of California at eleven thousand feet above sea level. Their stunted and tortured shapes, twisted like taffy by relentless winds, give little indication that they have endured almost five thousand years. Tundra plants survive the harsh climates of polar regions and high mountain peaks by hugging the ground in dwarf, compact masses. Like bonsai replicas of their cousins in more temperate latitudes, they disguise their true age with modest size.

Nature's mantle is visible in forest and meadow, city park and window-sill. It paints our world with rainbow hues of flowers and fruits, offering pleasure and sustenance for body and spirit. It can also be an environmental barometer, a miner's canary warning of impending dangers. Forests pale from deep emerald to sickly yellow as they die from acid rain; leaves spotted and speckled by airborne pollutants turn brown and fall to the ground, exposing the stark skeletons of barren trees.

Yet leafless brown does not always signal death; it sometimes denotes dormancy, a temporary state whose revitalization will be heralded by the spring quickening of buds and bark. Green, then, is the color of renewal and hope, an announcement of life. The actions of humans across the globe will determine whether it will prevail. One thing is certain: The disappearance of living green will foretell not only the end of plants, but of all plant-dependent species on earth, including humankind.

Green Nature's Continuum

In wilderness where humans do not tread, the constant interplay among inherent biologic and environmental elements creates a continuum of ecosystems. Although they may appear quiescent, each is an arena teeming with conflicting interests: plants best attuned to a particular site will survive and form a community reflective of that area's inherent qualities. Forest, savannah, prairie, meadow, swamp, marsh, or desert—the rich diversity of plant life displayed at any locale represents the current state of the ecological contest there.

Like the edges of a water-stained inkblot, wilderness blurs into human-created landscapes—farms, roads and railways, and living and working spaces. Crisscrossing the land, transportation systems provide expanding access between urban centers and rural areas.

To reach the city, we traverse suburbs framed by large shade trees. Here, green nature is often expressed in expansive lawns punctuated by shrubs that hide building foundations. Herbaceous flowering plants, massed in decorative edges and beds, leave the idiosyncratic fingerprint of each homeowner visible in their varied designs.

Closer to the urban core, lots become smaller and lawns and gardens shrink. Finally, the living soil is entombed beneath layers of asphalt and concrete, a canyon floor of streets and parking lots threaded around vertical buildings. Yet in every unclaimed niche, wherever sufficient light penetrates man-made structures, defiant nature breaks forth. Exuberant weeds seek out cracks in sidewalk, road, and curb.

In densely populated areas, where plants may be neglected, destroyed, or else carefully nurtured in discreet oases, green nature brings life to concrete, steel, glass, and asphalt. City parks provide sanctuaries, and an impression of continuous growth is created if trees and shrubs along roadways and plazas are regularly replaced. Severed from their roothold in native soil and transplanted to the city, plants stubbornly push new roots into earth substitutes. They unfurl their banners outside of buildings, clinging to walls, festooning windows and balconies, and transforming rooftops into verdant outposts. Within buildings they proclaim their message in flowerpots on windowsills and desks, along corridors, and at elevators. Echoes of larger landscapes are found in specially constructed atria in offices, hotels, restaurants, stores, shopping malls, and hospitals, where they provide protective habitats for lush displays of vegetation.

Such is the realm of green nature—from its home in the unpeopled wilderness to its precarious position as guest in an urban environment, totally dependent on human nurturing. But always, whether in majestic or miniature representation, plants signal the presence of an unremitting life energy that pulses throughout the universe.

THE HUMAN EXPERIENCE OF NATURE

Green nature enters human experience through innumerable childhood windows and is never entirely forgotten. Who has not searched for four-leaf clovers, omens of good luck, or pulled a grass blade free of its sheath and tasted the sweet, tender stem? The reflected glow of buttercups held beneath the chin reveals a fondness for butter, and daisies still determine "loves me, loves me not." Remember how it feels to ascend green slopes soft as fur and then roll downhill until sky and earth spin together in dizzy ecstasy? To blow white paratroops of dandelions against the wind and split their hollow stems into coiled springs? To achieve the raucous blare of a grass whistle stretched between paired thumbs? Children know that a weedy vacant lot can be a secret jungle hideout, filled with wild beasts and adventure, and that any bough large enough to bear one's weight must be climbed. For many each winter, fresh-cut Christmas trees bring starlight indoors with them and the cold fragrance of mysterious woods.

Green nature has been a silent companion to the ongoing drama of evolution. The human species was born into an environment already populated with a wide diversity of plants, which, during our shared evolutionary journey, have continually interacted with each other.

At first the limited population of hunter-gatherers made small impact on earth's vegetation; however, as humans settled into agricultural villages, they tamed and dominated the wild to serve the needs of their increasing numbers. In an ever-accelerating pattern that still continues, green nature has been beaten back and destroyed, its total area and complexity diminished as it succumbs to the relentless pressure of exploding humanity.

Yet, since emerging as a species, humans have been intensely curious about plants, subjecting them to observation and manipulation and classifying them by weight, color, scent, leaf shape, and arrangement. Plants are macerated and their juices extracted. They are peeled, boiled, broiled, ingested, planted, and transplanted. Their component parts are used to produce essentials such as food and luxuries such as perfumes. Leaves and other parts are collected, pressed, dried, sprayed, arranged in vases, and glued on plaques. Plants provide the basic raw materials for many musical instruments, both historic and modern. They yield substances that create altered mental states. Plant fibers are woven, braided, dyed for cloth, and turned into placemats, doormats, and hats. They form the substance of the pages in this book.

Examples of literature, art, music, medicine, and cooking document the countless ways that plants intersect with human culture. More important, the two life forms are joined in ways that denote an even closer relationship than most people suspect: Scientists have found that the chlorophyll molecules of green plants bear an intriguing similarity to hemoglobin, the prime constituent of mammalian blood. Both are composed of a ring of carbon and nitrogen atoms surrounding a single atom. Their difference lies in the central atom, which is magnesium in chlorophyll and iron in hemoglobin. The similarity of these two essential biological components suggests a common origin somewhere in the primordial soup where life began on earth.

Green plants are the earth's lungs. They produce oxygen and consume carbon dioxide, thus making existence possible for humans and all other forms of life, which, by contrast, inhale oxygen and expel carbon dioxide. Another way plants are fundamental to the continuance of life on this planet is through their ability to transform and store energy. Each day the sun bathes the earth with energy equal to 684 billion tons of coal. Most of this abundance is quickly lost, reflected back into the darkness of outer space. However, the sunlight that falls on chlorophyll-producing plants can be entrapped through photosynthesis and transmuted to more stable forms, holding the energy on earth for a while before it ultimately is released.

Barely 2 percent of the total sunlight striking green plants is absorbed, and only half of that is in wave lengths usable for photosynthesis. The incredible fact is that only 1 percent of the total sunlight reaching it drives the whole living portion of earth's biosphere.

This energy flows through the entire food chain. Sun-powered photosynthesis removes carbon dioxide from the atmosphere, extracts the carbon, and recombines it into the carbohydrates, proteins, and fats necessary to create leaves, stems, roots, and seeds. These become food for another level of animal: herbivores who eat the plants, thereby acquiring some of the original solar energy that was entrapped. Still higher on the chain are human beings—omnivores who eat both plants and the animals who have eaten the plants. In other words, the solar energy originally captured by plants moves through our veins, powering us and firing our metabolism to maintain a stable body temperature of 98.7° F.

Millions of years ago, plants, with their locked-in store of carbon, buried under extremely high temperatures and pressure, were metamorphosed into coal, gas, and oil. Today, we burn these fuels to heat our homes and run our machinery. In each case, the heat imprisoned by plants, having served our human purposes, is finally freed to drift out into the earth's atmosphere.

Unfortunately, combustion also releases a huge quantity of carbon dioxide, which is now enveloping the planet, creating a potential disaster by blocking dissipation of heat to the outer atmosphere—the "greenhouse effect." To solve this problem, scientists look to photosynthesis, which ties up the gas in plant tissue. We are urged to maximize the number of woody plants on earth through programs for planting trees, preventing further destruction of forests, and encouraging reforestation all over the world. But, as usual, there is a catch. Because the earth's surface has cooled and volcanic activity is minimal, trees that remove carbon dioxide from the atmosphere today will not be entombed to become fossil fuels. Rather, when they fall and decay, they will release into the air all their stored solar energy, and with it the carbon dioxide they originally removed

from the atmosphere. Lest these plants produce the very problem of global warming they were meant to prevent, replacement of trees must remain an ongoing process. Only continued replanting will ensure the balance between carbon dioxide being removed from the air by living
chlorophyll and energy released by the decaying of dead vegetation.

Although vegetation's role in sustaining physical mammalian life is
fairly well understood, one aspect has remained unexplored: In what ways
do plants in their myriad forms enter our mental and spiritual lives? What
are the subtle meanings assigned to green nature by the human psyche?

Bringing the Outside Inside

Because my primary concern is to explore how the presence of green
nature affects people, I will here examine human-plant relationships—
particularly at a psychological level. Plants exist as part of the familiar
three-dimensional environment; however, before they can affect people
emotionally, they must be incorporated into the inner mental world.

How can this be done? We identify physical objects, including plants and
landscapes, by characteristics such as size, shape, color, and weight. While
assessing these qualities, we simultaneously file a mental record of our experience with objects and of any feelings that might have occurred during
encounters with them. The quality of those experiences, then, becomes
subconsciously associated with the objects. In later meetings, images of the
objects will prod us mentally to sample those stored thoughts and feelings,
which will then determine how we interpret the objects.

Poets have long sung of such personal reactions to nature. Wordsworth,
for example, writes, "My heart leaps up when I behold a rainbow in the
sky."[1] Seeing the physical reality—a multicolored arc—caused his response, "my heart leaps up," even before he had intellectually compre-
hended the rainbow.

It is the split second during which we *feel* before we *know* that provides
insight into a different way of knowing, one that is intuitive rather than
cognitive. The rainbow is in the sky, but the up-leaping heart is in the poet;
the visual image is internalized and comes to life as personal experience.
Clearly, the rainbow's meaning lies beyond the mere physics of the color
spectrum. To Wordsworth, emotion is more significant than any refrac-
tion of the sun's rays by raindrops. Frederick Law Olmsted, father of
American landscape architecture, was well aware of feelings evoked by
landscapes. "The chief purpose of a park was 'its effect on the human

organism . . . like that of music . . . that goes back of thought and cannot be fully given in the form of words.'"[2] He strove to invoke such feelings when designing his parks, knowing that our emotional response to what we see adds richness and quality to everyday experiences.

Bridging the gap between what is internal and what is external is the function of our senses. They convey messages from the three-dimensional world into the complex corridors of our mind, that subconscious matrix through which all we see must pass. We need to examine the dichotomy between what we are within the envelope of our skin and everything else that lies beyond that boundary. Inside, we are bone, sinew, organs, and complex liquids pulsing through tissue. Outside is the rest of the world—other people, objects, buildings, and landscapes. We can escape our somatic prison only through sensory perception of what exists beyond it, and green nature is an important part of that beyond.

To clarify the distinction between a physical object and its mental translation in our brain, we can compare our eyes with a camera. In both eye and camera, light enters the lens and an inverted image is presented. In a camera, the inverted image is recorded on film, which is then processed to produce a negative, the reverse picture of what came through the lens.

Different cameras, photographing the same subject, using the same location, lighting, and film, and developed with the same procedures, will produce virtually identical images. But people are not cameras. Two individuals looking at the same object under the same conditions will rarely experience identical responses. Human vision is personal, intimately bound up with all that has ever happened to us. It is tied to our psyche, reservoir for everything we know.

In our eye, the inverted image comes to rest on the retina, the optical outpost of the brain, a living interface between outside and inside.[3] The retina translates the inverted visual image into electrical impulses and neurochemical transmitters, an internal language the body uses to communicate with itself. Messages describing what has been seen race through neural pathways to inform the brain, where the three-dimensional object becomes a stimulus for feelings and emotions such as pleasure, fear, or curiosity.

GREEN NATURE: A POINT OF VIEW

Eyes are like machines for gathering light, allowing us to see. But vision, making sense of that light, is a function of the brain and neurological systems. Zen masters teach that one must look beyond the "fingers point-ing at the moon," lest they distract us from the moon itself. In this way, we should learn to see plants as more than material objects. They are as-pects of a universal life force.

So long as our sight is limited to visualizing trees and other plants as objects, our view is deflected. But when we look beyond individual forms, when we comprehend plants as interconnected elements of a larger de-sign in which people are also a thread, then we have the opportunity to understand our part in the complex tapestry of life.

This broadened perspective is often found in gardening. At some point during the long process, we begin to realize that *we* do not grow the plants. They grow of themselves in response to their own genetic rhythm. We participate by nurturing—adjusting nutrients, water, and light to permit optimum expression of the plant's potential. Gardening teaches us that we cannot always have our own way and yet allows us to feel good about that reality. Is that not the truth of human development as well? Both plants and humans are parts of the total web of life in which all living things participate and of which we are merely one strand.

We can begin to see the continuity of green nature with human nature when we use green nature as a lens through which to focus on our role in the natural environment. The feelings it engenders can be guides that help us understand our interconnectedness.

NATURE AND CULTURE

Western civilization it seems, has an overriding purpose: to free us from reliance on natural forces, allowing us to fashion our own world and cre-ate our own future.[4] Proof of our accomplishments surrounds us: cities' complex structures and the myriad devices that allow them to function; electronic umbilicals that tie us together with sight and sound and the abilities to cut through mountains, redirect rivers, walk on the moon, and harness powers of the atom. This is the technological stuff of our civili-zation, where each new invention reassures us that we are no longer im-potent servants of unpredictable nature. Barbara Ward and René DuBos identify the two worlds in which we dwell as the "biosphere of our inher-itance and the technosphere of our creation."[5]

Throughout history, cautionary words have been spoken and written to temper our hubris. For as long as people have interacted with land-scape, writers and storytellers have reminded us "of the breadth of the universe and the inability of the individual mind to encompass what is known or what can be known."⁶ We are warned that green nature and all it represents is neither an enemy nor a servant to be subjugated.

Thoreau at Walden Pond, and Aldo Leopold in *Sand County Almanac* have spoken eloquently of our linkage to nature and the land. Ian McHarg, a landscape architect, in *Design with Nature* proposed a design concept respectful of natural constraints.⁷ McHarg retells a fable from Loren Eiseley: "Man in space is enabled to look upon the distant earth, a celestial orb, a revolving sphere. He sees it to be green, from the verdure on the land, algae greening the oceans, a green celestial fruit. Looking closely at earth, he perceives blotches, black, brown, gray, and from these extend dynamic tentacles upon the green epidermis. These blemishes he recognizes as the cities and works of man and asks, 'Is man but a planetary disease?'"

We sit perched on a limb that supports our physiological and psychological well-being, and heedlessly, with deft strokes, we are sawing off that limb behind ourselves.

2

$\sim$

Green Nature and Human Evolution

We should consider how "our aesthetic reactions to landscapes may have derived, in part, from an evolved psychology that functioned to help hunter-gatherers make better decisions about when to move, where to settle, and what activities to follow in various localities . . . stimuli such as flowers, sunsets, clouds, thunder, snakes and lions activate response systems of ancient origin."[1]

We think we know ourselves: We are decision-making individuals who analyze situations, puzzle through problems, and arrive at solutions. Then, during the course of an ordinary day, something might happen that suddenly reveals the presence of another self within us. This hidden self is not controlled by conscious thought, but acts spontaneously on the basis of intuitive wisdom. Generally, we pay no attention to these reflexive actions because they do not engage our intellect, but by ignoring them we do ourselves a disservice. We miss an opportunity to discover connections to other life on earth and our role in the total design.

Like the tip of an iceberg, our other self floats at the edge of our awareness, responding to stimuli, repairing damage, adjusting and maintaining internal systems, and keeping us alive. Persons in whom these automatic responses are missing or malfunctioning usually suffer a difficult and abbreviated existence.

The hidden self signals its presence in many ways. When we are startled by an unexpected sound—the shatter of falling glass, the honk of an automobile horn—adrenaline is released, and our hearts pound in an instantaneous, unconscious act. At a lecture, we focus on the speaker; yet, should another figure appear at one side of the stage, our eyes will automatically shift to the newcomer. For many, encounters with spiders, snakes, or other creatures evoke a spontaneous sense of revulsion. We may even feel the hairs on our head "stand up" or "goose bumps" rise along our arms.

The hidden self can react to what is seen or sensed—a landscape, a person, or a sound—with instant feelings of like or dislike. Such intuitions, not the result of consciously directed thought, are "wired" into us and belong to an inherent physiological and psychological blueprint unique to each individual. These responses often make no practical sense in a contemporary context; they are reminders that our origin as a species was not in the contemporary world.

Our modern intellectual persona inhabits a physical body programmed in primitive times. Its responses to stimuli reflect signals of early stages of evolution that are today often inappropriate and sometimes damaging. For example, the "fight or flee" response that pours adrenaline into the bloodstream when we are startled or angry can cause high blood pressure, stroke, and other insults to the cardiovascular system.

We can help harmonize our physical and hidden selves and reduce the stress that results from denying their separate needs by seeking to understand the remote origins of these automatic behaviors. How might they have helped the first Homo sapiens survive in a hostile environment? On one level, they are the product of body knowledge—wisdom accumulated through eons of evolution and encoded in our genes. Our bodies, acting without our conscious instruction, continuously perform a multitude of functions to maintain internal homeostasis. Pain, thirst, and hunger are signals of this body knowledge, alerting us to critical physical needs.

Body wisdom often senses what is required and reacts immediately; when we cut a finger, for example, we do not knowingly order actions to stop the bleeding, create a scab, and reconnect severed tissue. When we see the wound, our blood pressure drops automatically, reducing the danger of excessive loss. Antibodies rush to the site, clotting factors stanch the bleeding and form a protective covering, and the growth of new skin cells is accelerated. If we had to think about each step, we would probably bleed to death rather than heal.

Recognizing the hidden self's intrinsic role in daily survival makes us wonder where else this ancient individual might be at work. Some psychologists believe that emotional responses to nature settings are the psychic equivalent of body knowledge. They find that we feel less stressed when viewing scenes of green nature rather than urban settings of buildings, streets, and traffic. A walk in the woods can refresh the spirit, and gardens have long been recognized as sources of peacefulness. Such positive human responses occur consistently across social, economic, and racial boundaries.

There are ancient echoes in our attraction to blazing fall color (cold weather is coming, must stockpile food and move on to more sheltered areas) or the bright, fragrant blossoms of spring (fresh food and water will soon be plentiful, warmer days will bring more game). These visceral reactions surely played an important role in our ancestral survival and perhaps, like body knowledge, were locked in our genes as we evolved.

Evolution: People and Plants

Life for an individual begins at birth, but when does life begin for a species? Humans represent but a blip in the grand scale of planetary evolution. Richard H. Wagner, a biologist, places us in a proper perspective: "If you were to consider evolution of life on earth as a thirty-minute film, you would see wave after wave of new species evolving, filling the environment with a diversity of life forms, and then receding—sometimes totally, but occasionally leaving a few of the best adapted species behind. It is humbling to note that man's existence on earth would flash by in the last 3.5 seconds of that film!"[2]

Before mammals appeared, however, primitive plant forms were already thriving in primordial seas. During 2.5 billion years of evolution, plants moved from the water to colonize the land. Earth's early atmosphere, rich in carbon dioxide, was ideal for more advanced stationary life forms that could obtain their essential nutrients—carbon dioxide and a solution of salts—while rooted in one place.

Plants expand their dominion through growth, extending upward and outward from their fixed spot, or they throw seeds and spores that ride the wind. But over millennia, other life forms evolved that required living food for sustenance and had to move about to obtain it. Those animals developed skeletal and muscular structures that enhanced their mobility and differentiated sense organs that aided their search for food in the surrounding environment. Impulses originating in these organs were coordinated and transmitted through increasingly complex nervous systems to activate appropriate muscular responses.

In addition to instinctive responses, the progenitors of modern humans developed a large brain, which gave them the capacity to analyze situations, make decisions, and plan for the future. Such reasoning ability was critical to survival, for in an environment that could both sustain and threaten it was important to learn to distinguish settings that offered positive opportunities. Lacking a guide book, humans were forced to seek subtle environmental clues that spelled survival or danger. The green environment itself became their library, providing information on its suitability for nurturing human life. Success in reading the landscape became their passport to join those who continued the species.

Mammals and birds still display instinctive nesting and courting behaviors developed during their long evolutionary journey. Why should there not be remnants of similar behaviors in human beings? In recent years, an interdisciplinary group of scientists has worked to tease out the "green thread" common to us all. By following this thread, we can become aware of our connections to nature and see them as integral parts of our humanity.

LANDSCAPE PREFERENCES

How do we examine our ancient past? The stones and bones that archaeologists, anthropologists, and historians study tell us how we looked, what we built, the societies we developed, and the events that moved us through history. But the role of our nonphysical selves—how we thought, felt, and reacted in a primitive environment, things "not revealed by artifacts"—is under exploration by a small group of geographers and environmental psychologists. They seek contemporary patterns of responses shared across social, economic, cultural, and racial boundaries. When identified, these commonalities can be attributed to some primitive root in the human psyche rather than to contemporary cultural conditioning. Human preferences for specific landscape configurations are one example.

One way to explore landscape preferences is to show people slides, carefully controlled for content, ranging from totally urban to untouched wilderness settings. As the slides flash briefly on the screen, viewers are asked to indicate the attractiveness of each scene on a scale of one to five. Researchers quickly found that urban scenes lacking in trees, shrubs, or grass receive uniformly low ratings, whereas the mere presence of vegetation enhances the appeal of a slide.[3] Despite the fact that humans have created massive technological landscapes, many cross-cultural studies show that we instinctively crave natural features in our surroundings.

Although its very presence is a desired trait, patterns in vegetation also strongly influence the way people rate landscapes. The spatial arrangement of plants, rocks, and water courses is an important factor in making a landscape attractive. We prefer diversity over a single species, a mixed border rather than a cornfield, an open woods rather than one dense with underbrush. We also seek a sense of order, whether natural or constructed, choosing the carefully arranged stones of a Japanese garden over a pile of rocks in a field.

Rachel Kaplan and Stephen Kaplan, who are environmental psychologists, have identified four qualities that aid in decoding a landscape. The first is coherence, the ease with which one can grasp the organization of the landscape, that is, how well it hangs together. Is it a random scattering of rocks, or are the rocks part of a carefully designed meditation garden? The second, legibility, concerns whether the third dimension is apparent. How well would one find one's way into and out of the setting? Complexity, the third quality, concerns whether the scene displays diversity or contains a limited number of different objects. The final, most important, quality is mystery, the promise of new information if one could explore farther into the landscape. This is the tantalizing call that urges viewers to try to see beyond the path curving out of sight or to gain a better view of the building partially screened by vegetation. It is mystery that piques curiosity about what further information might be learned. The presence of mystery is identified as the most consistent predictor of landscape preference.[4]

Roger Ulrich, also an enviromental psychologist, analyzes landscape preference by measuring physiological and psychophysiological responses—heart rate, blood pressure, muscle tension, and brain waves.[5] He confirms that viewing preferred settings measurably reduces tension and enhances recovery from stressful situations. In one study, students who had just completed an examination were divided into two sections. Ulrich showed nature scenes to one group, urban scenes to the other. Those shown nature scenes exhibited lowered stress, whereas students viewing urban scenes became even more tense than when they had emerged from the examination.

Ulrich cites six variables that affect the informational qualities of a landscape and thereby its preference rating: focality is a setting, which includes a point that draws attention and is the logical place from which

A path curving out of sight, which invites further exploration, is highly preferred. (Author's photo)

A straight path, which reveals all at a glance, is less preferred. (Author's photo)

to begin visual assessment; complexity is the moderate-to-high variety of elements that constitutes the setting but allows the presence of pattern; depth is the openness that allows one to see into the landscape; ground texture is the evenness that implies easy navigation through the setting; deflected vista is the idea that entering the scene would reveal more information than can be seen; and appraised threat is the sense that danger is negligible or absent.[6]

From analyses of the way landscapes provide information, these researchers conclude that humans, in order to operate effectively, must be inherently able to interpret the cues in their immediate environment and infer what is likely to occur as they move within it. The rapidity and ease of judging landscapes and the similar results among participants of widely varying backgrounds have led scientists to see "preference as an expression of an intuitive guide to behavior, an inclination to make choices which would lead the individual away from inappropriate environments and toward desirable ones."[7] When questioned, participants are not able to explain why certain settings attract them more than others. The choice comes from feeling ("my heart leaps up") rather than conscious thought, but the remarkably similar results of studies across different cultures support the idea that an important biological factor is involved.

Throughout human history, landscape preference flows like a stream that is reinterpreted as it passes through each culture. The geographer Jay Appleton has presented a theory of preference based on the ability of a setting to offer prospect, a broad view of the surrounding area, and at the same time afford refuge, that is, protection from being seen by others.[8] This type of setting (such as the edge of the woods, where one could watch approaching animals yet still be hidden from their sight) would indeed be advantageous for primitive humans. Appleton also traces the expression of prospect and refuge in seventeenth- and eighteenth-century paintings and architecture, showing how they demonstrate cultural interpretations of these underlying innate preferences.[9]

The constancy of specific preferences across broadly diverse populations leads psychologists to believe that preference denotes a basic human characteristic. Because we are information-processing beings—taking in what we find through our senses, interpreting and using the information as a basis for decisions—it follows that landscape preferences must be connected with this human ability and communicate something meaningful. Landscape preference is now understood to be a remnant of the adaptive behavior that helped establish the species.

Like two threads, innate and culturally induced needs are warp and woof of the human fabric. Using a piece of fine brocade as example, the bewildering confusion of pattern becomes comprehensible when the cloth is turned over; its reverse side exposes the intricate weave that forms the design. So, with humans, we must devise a method to separate inborn responses from contemporary cultural influences. A preference for nature scenes is one of the threads that can lead us back to our ancient selves and provide access to the origin of those feelings.

Making Sense Out of What Is Seen

At some point, probably in the African savanna, our ancestors descended from the trees to dwell on the ground. They moved from a multidimensional arboreal life, with its opportunities to traverse freely up, down, or sideways, to a single-plane environment that demanded extreme readjustment of their learned behavior.

Intruders in a savanna already inhabited, the new arrivals were forced to depend on their intelligence to outwit the resident populations. Although slower of foot than many other animals, physically smaller and lacking claws and fangs, their larger brain capacity enabled them to plan responses to almost any possible situation. "Under these circumstances, figuring out what might happen well before it did happen was not merely useful; it was essential."[10]

Earthbound bipeds soon learned that there was safety in numbers. During the Stone Age (ca. 1,000,000 B.C. to 12,000 B.C.), humans formed primitive social organizations, joining together in hunter-gatherer groups whose life was a long, precarious camping trip with no permanent abode. Abundance of food and water was a limiting factor; when local supplies ran out, the group would move on. The ability to interpret clues in the landscape as indications of the availability of food, water, and shelter was essential; those most skilled in finding life-sustaining resources lived and were able to transmit their genes to the next generation. Through trial and error, repeated observation and analysis, they learned to recognize and prefer environmental features that suggested safety and to avoid those that offered danger, forming these judgments as they migrated across earth's broad variety of ecosystems. Our ancestors were dependent on this way of seeking existential amenities in the landscape until as recently as five hundred generations ago.[11]

Because life's ultimate criterion is its own perpetuation, there must be close links between the survival of Homo sapiens and the primitive green environment in which we evolved. We can, with some confidence, reconstruct the scene where humans first appeared on the planet, what they found, and what they required to flourish and reproduce. Success in selecting a favorable habitat, essential for survival, would have been an intense and time-consuming activity for hunter-gatherers. While studying the potential of a landscape, they could easily have been surprised by unseen dangers that crawled, roamed, or slithered in the surrounding environment. Thus it would have been an evolutionary advantage for them to learn to quickly recognize the characteristics of a viable habitat, to know that the presence and shape of certain plants would indicate the abundance or absence of water, shelter, or food.

Learning is a complex process that involves more than pure thought; humans also are informed by emotions and sensations. When we feel hunger or thirst, we seek food or drink; when we feel pain, we cry out or quickly recoil. Emotions and sensations are noncognitive ways of being aware, and they are part of the equipment primitive humans evolved that reinforces distinct types of behavior. By rewarding success with positive emotional responses, an individual is encouraged to repeat enjoyable activities—whether it be selecting a safe habitat, eating, drinking, or having sex. Negative emotional responses, on the other hand, discourage repetition of behavior that causes danger or pain.

That is how those who lived to become our ancestors must have developed their ability to judge a setting viscerally. Selection of successful habitats would have been enhanced by the pleasant feelings engendered there; they would have learned to select an environment because it "felt" good. Relying on instinctive feelings to first evaluate a site would have freed their minds to plan further action or deal with potential enemies lurking in the area.

Acquiring any new skill demands intense concentration, particularly at the start. But once that skill is comfortably part of our abilities, executing it becomes automatic. What we have absorbed resides within our body knowledge and does not require constant attention. When learning to drive a car, for example, we must first focus on each move: steering, shifting, accelerating, decelerating, and avoiding other objects. All our mental faculties are centered on controlling the beast, and we despair of ever conquering it. (That is why large signs adorn student-driver vehicles.) However, once we have learned the steps, we find that we can attend to other things, listen to the radio, glimpse the scenery, or converse with a passenger. Driving becomes largely an automatic response to input received by the senses.

So site selection must have become automatic for Homo sapiens. In addition, if the ability to assess a setting intuitively was encoded into the genes, it would not have to be learned anew by each individual. Transgenerational transfer of this information would be accomplished in the same way that norms of heartbeat or body temperature are passed on as a component of every healthy newborn. This, too seems to have occurred during our long evolution.

It is clear, however, that our underlying ability to assess a landscape is not as fixed as our normal heartbeat. The genetic component may be set, but cultural overlay influences its expression. Each of us responds within a context of our own life experience. Thus, both cultural and genetic components are involved when we view a site and intuitively know whether or not we like it.

LANDSCAPE OF SAVANNA

Because our humanoid predecessors are believed to have originated in the savannas of Africa, Gordon Orians and Judith Heerwagen have studied that biome (a community of plants and animals that live together in a large geographic region having a certain kind of climate) to determine which of its characteristics might have offered the best opportunities for survival.[12]

Savanna is an open landscape of scattered trees with an understory of grasses and shrubs that affords distant views for safety as well as clear surveillance of the immediate neighborhood. There are enough trees to give protection from weather and ground-based predators, and food sources both for people and grazing animals are adequate.

Certain species of trees can indicate the presence of water, which is relatively scarce and unpredictably distributed on African savannas. Orians and Heerwagen have studied savanna tree types and found that the shape of the fine-leafed, widespread *Acacia tortilis* varies according to the availability of moisture. "In high quality habitat, this acacia has the quintessential savanna look—a spreading multi-layered canopy and a trunk that branches close to the ground. In wetter [overly moist] savannas, the species develops a canopy that is taller than it is broad with high trunk, while in dry savanna *A. tortilis* is dense and shrubby looking."[13] Thus, a savanna with umbrella-shaped trees branched low to the ground would

Acacia tortilis achieves a distinctive shape in adequately moist habitats. (Courtesy of Elizabeth Orians)

signal a habitat that had the proper amount of moisture to sustain life. This was a survivor's landscape, and the ability to recognize it quickly would have been a powerful asset to primitive humans roaming the area.

If dwellers in the savanna did use tree shapes and the visual appearance of the terrain for swift assessment of its potential as a habitat, could they not have evolved innate preferences for particular landscape characteristics (preferences that resonate within us to this day)? Apparently so. Researchers have found that Americans like park settings that might be characterized as "savannas," featuring a ground cover of grass, no tangled underbrush, and broad, open spacing of mature trees.[14] Anthropologists sometimes refer to savanna as "parkland."

Further confirmation of our ongoing savanna preference is found in a study by psychologist John D. Balling and ecologist John Falk.[15] Participants lived in an East Coast area characterized by temperate deciduous forest and represented a broad spectrum: third-graders, sixth-graders, college students, adults, senior citizens, and professional foresters. Each group was shown slides typical of five different biomes—tropical rain forest, temperate deciduous forest, coniferous forest, savanna, and desert—and asked to rate the setting in terms of how much they would like to live in or visit a similar area. The third- and sixth-graders (eight and eleven years old) expressed significant preference for savanna over all other biomes. For all older participants, however, familiar natural environments were equally favored with savanna.

Because none of the youngsters had ever actually seen a savanna, the researchers conclude that their expressed preference indicates that "humans have an innate preference for savanna-like settings that arises from their long evolutionary history on the savannas of East Africa."[16] Only as people grow older do they begin to select more varied landscapes. In other words, it seems that children are born with a preference for savanna; it is encoded in their genes.

This thought is echoed by Richard Leakey, son of famed African anthropologists Mary and Louis Leakey, who, when asked why Africa has so profound an effect on people, replied, "Genetic memory . . . the vast majority of people who come here feel something they feel nowhere else. It is not the wildlife, it is the place. If, as I believe, it is a memory, almost a familiarity, it is very primitive. It is the capacity homing pigeons have, salmon have, to recognize, to go back. You feel it's home. It feels right to be here."[17]

Gordon Orians and Judith Heerwagen showed slides of *Acacia tortilis* to respondents from Seattle, Argentina, and Australia and found that all groups rated as most attractive trees that have moderately dense canopies and multiple trunks originating near the ground. Trees with high trunks and either sparse or very dense canopies are judged as less attractive. The selected trees are typical of the shape of *Acacia tortilis* growing in adequately moist soils.

It is likely that the trees and shrubs we choose for our gardens echo our inborn preferences for certain contours. Orians has studied woody plants used in Japan, where the art of making gardens is very old.[18] Because the Japanese use few flowers, beauty in their landscapes is created primarily from the shapes and arrangements of nonflowering trees and shrubs. Orians has searched for evidence that the Japanese are influenced by innate preferences for the tree profiles of the African savanna, and he notes that maples (*Acer*) are frequently used in plantings. Wild species of maples chosen for landscaping tend to be broader than they are high, with shorter trunks and smaller, more deeply divided leaves than species that are rejected. In Japanese gardens, maples generally grow unpruned and are allowed to achieve their natural shapes. Even in selecting oaks (*Quercus*), small-leaved, evergreen species are preferred over large-leaved, deciduous ones.

The only Japanese conifer that achieves a spreading character in its native habitat is the red pine, which, in windswept locations, develops a layered, horizontal form. Yet most conifers in Japanese gardens are rigorously pruned to create evergreens with a distinctly layered aspect, a canopy broader than tall, and trunks that branch close to the ground. The horizontal shape is emphasized by supporting, low-spreading branches to permit an unusually long extension of growth. All these characteristics recall savanna trees.

OTHER CLUES FOR SURVIVAL

While pursuing day-to-day affairs, concentrating on the work at hand, it would have been critical for primitive humans to recognize cues portending events of great importance. If the cue signaled danger or a sudden change, an immediate response would have been needed, overriding any momentary preoccupation. This would be much the same as a fire alarm or air raid warning today. From an evolutionary viewpoint, alarm cues would be most effective if they aroused a powerful emotional reaction, drawing attention even more strongly to the cue.

One could say that human emotional responses evolved in part to underscore information that enabled our primitive ancestors to function more effectively. Cues that signified a change in weather would have been particularly important, because perhaps they would indicate an event for which one would have to prepare. Some, like cloud formations, wind, or sudden alterations in temperature, would demand immediate action, such as relocating to find refuge from an impending storm.

Other cues signal happenings that occur more slowly and are not of such urgency. Indicators foretelling a change of season, for example, would initiate a longer preparation period than those needed to escape a passing thunder storm. Those who live by hunting or gathering, fishing or farming, must observe nature's signs—the angle of the sun, the waning of the moon, the position of the stars—to know when to plant and when to harvest, when to move to summer pasture or seek winter shelter. Changes in foliage color would be a strong indication that preparations for surviving the long winter should begin.

Environmental alarm bells once set off behaviors in our primitive ancestors that helped them to survive, and those alarms continue to sound within us. We are sensitive to the onset of afternoon and night, and sunrise and sunset remain deeply fascinating. For an animal with poor night vision, such signals would be cues to seek shelter from the coming darkness or to prepare for a new day. We are endlessly enthralled by the shapes of clouds; poets and painters use their skill to portray them to us. But our ancient ancestors read the clouds as omens and for information about wind, weather, water, and shade.

Each spring, trees leaf out, grass sprouts, flowers bloom, and we feel relief and joy in life's renewal. In autumn's annual ritual, millions head for the countryside to view the spectacle of forests turning orange, red, yellow, and purple. These pilgrims ride bumper to bumper along New England roads or through the Smoky Mountains. Most could observe the changing colors in their own backyards, yet they feel compelled to find a "natural" place to immerse themselves in beauty with few reminders of the constructed world in which they spend their daily lives.

Poets and writers are aware of the emotions hidden in our experience with nature. Just as Wordsworth experienced the rainbow, Annie Dillard tells of a cedar transfigured, "the tree with lights in it."[19] She is awestruck and struggles to describe the feelings that arise from this transitory confrontation with nature.

Other signals, adaptive for primitive humans, still resonate within us. Fire retains its life or death significance. Confined in a fireplace or a camp circle, it is warm and comforting. One can gaze, mesmerized by flames that shift like the beating of brilliant wings. That same fire, uncontrolled, consuming buildings, forest, and field, becomes a voracious monster that demands fear and yet still exerts its powerful fascination.

Early humans would have had to be highly sensitive to the presence of large or fierce predators that could threaten their lives. Immediate awareness would have given them a better chance to climb to safety or prepare to kill the animal. Many people still participate in hunting rituals, seeking to experience the mystical bond between stalker and prey which exists in indigenous cultures and which interpreters find expressed in the ancient cave paintings of Lascaux or rock art of the American Southwest. Others flock to zoos and safari parks, responding to the deep, complex bonds we have developed over the millennia with other creatures.

Our love of flowers, too, is undoubtedly of ancient origin. In an otherwise green and brown world, flowers might have served as vibrant flags, locating sources of food. Perhaps that is why modern hybridization often results in more striking forms and hues—doubles, large blooms, bicolor, and multicolor—that make the flower more easily apprehended. Excavation of Neanderthal burial sites in Iraq has revealed an abundance of pollen grains in each grave, a sign that flowers were part of that final act of mortal recognition.[20] Some scientists theorize that the purpose of the flowers was purely practical—allowing the dead to carry a kind of sustenance into the next world. But perhaps it reflected a basic response that we also share: Might these creatures not have loved flowers simply because they were beautiful?

This digression into evolution and the deeply rooted origin of contemporary landscape preferences is important in order to grasp the thesis of this book. In the following chapters, I will discuss how people respond to green nature in its many manifestations and its strong effects on their emotional well-being. Understanding the evolutionary perspective allows us to see that these responses are not fleeting or superficial; they reflect the presence within each of us of a continuous genetic link with green nature, from which our species learned how to survive. Awareness of the evolutionary origin of landscape preference recalls the concluding lines of Wordsworth's "The Rainbow":

> So was it when my life began;
> So is it now I am a man;
> So be it when I shall grow old,
>   Or let me die!
> The Child is the father of the Man;
> And I would wish my days to be
> Bound each to each by natural piety.[21]

Become consciously aware of the encoded meanings of green nature. When you stroll through gardens, grow plants, enjoy a walk in park or forest, know and heed the ancient child that was our parent. Still living within us, it continues to lead us along verdant paths of survival.

3

Green Nature Observed

The immense contribution gardens make to our cultural well-being cannot be measured but will always be felt. A visit to a garden is a visceral experience, a universal one at that, no language barrier exists. Here the eye, heart, and spirit do all the translating for us.[1]

How do we experience objects or respond to a particular place? For most of us, the first impression is through sight. We translate the inverted images apprehended by our retinas into our subconscious language, turning the three-dimensional world into a mental landscape and annotating it with nuances of personal meaning. What is observed is not separable from the observer; the filter of experience colors everything we see.

Our idea of a setting is filed in our psyche when we experience the sensual potpourri of sights, sounds, aromas, and tactile sensations that help tell us where we are. In cities, traffic clogs the streets, tainting the air with exhaust fumes and irritating smog. People intent on personal missions push past us on the pavement, shoes thumping on its hard surface. Hemmed in by buildings, our vision is restricted to the street on which we walk or to a piece of sky above; only at corners can we see in all directions.

Suburban sidewalks are equally unforgiving underfoot, but we can stray off the concrete to saunter through grass, feel the cushioned soil beneath, and smell its cool sweetness. The air is fresher and sun and shade alternate, not because buildings obstruct the light but because trees offer soothing shadow. Farthest from the city, in a landscape of field and forest, the prospect is green; earth's surface may be yielding or rocky and uneven. Sounds and fragrances from natural sources envelop us as we walk along.

In addition to sensory experiences, personal responses to specific objects are affected by cultural backgrounds. One example is the diverse reaction to *Ailanthus altissima,* the tree-of-heaven. American nursery owners and landscape architects reject this weedy denizen of city and suburb as being too coarse and rampant for use in designed landscapes. But in the inner city, where *Ailanthus* sprouts from every opportune cranny, residents identify it as a survivor that persists without outside nurturing. They welcome its dappled shelter from intense summer heat and the shifting visual relief its ragged foliage offers from the rigid structures of a city block. In the Netherlands and Korea, *Ailanthus* has an even better reputation and is actively promoted as a desirable street tree. It's the same plant, but the varying responses to *Ailanthus altissima* are determined by the cultural overlay and personal experiences that each viewer brings to it.

In another example, most people see vegetation in a city as a positive presence, ameliorating urban harshness. Others perceive low tree branches and dense shrubbery in public parks or near buildings as hiding places for muggers. To alleviate such anxiety, foliage is often removed in response to citizen pressure.

For me, the most dramatic example of the way cultural experience can affect the response to green nature occurred when I was leading a group of Chicago's inner-city youngsters on a field trip in the Morton Arboretum.[2] I was astonished to discover that they were terrified by the prospect of walking into the woods, a setting dearly loved by most arboretum visitors. Lack of personal contact with this type of landscape and years of associating "woods" with "jungle" made them fear they would be attacked by lions and tigers. It was only by helping them discover analogies between the structures and inhabitants of the forest and those of their own neighborhoods that I was able to put them at ease. The visit was a revelation for all of us. It made me aware of the fact that I, without a guide to interpret, would probably have been equally frightened to enter the crowded city turf that was their familiar playground.

Imagine how personal meanings influence the creation of a planned landscape: Concepts originate in the designer's mind, are translated into drawings, then fulfilled in three-dimensional reality on the ground. However, the process is still not complete. Only when people interact with the newly planted landscape, transforming the physical design into personal experience, is the circle closed. It is this final aspect—the synthesis that takes place in the minds of those who see it—that is of particular interest. The interplay of thought, experience, and meaning has always been present. Historically, garden styles have often reflected human and social influences.

In the mid-seventeenth century, Louis XIV built a garden in which every detail speaks of the grandeur and power of a single person—himself, *le roi du soleil.* The plan of Versailles is a metaphor for the society of the king's time. Only from the elevated vantage point of the palace windows can one view the entire landscape: tapestries where colored stones enhance the delicate horticultural stitching of parterres, long canals, waterworks, statuary, and paths that create a magnificent geometry. Nowhere is there any implication that natural forces created the garden. It is obviously the work of humans, the genius of Andre Le Notre in particular. At ground level, the garden awes visitors by its scale, which makes humans seem insignificant. Nature is constrained, bent, sheared into angular shapes; only within the strict confines of paths, parterres, canals, and pools are elements of vegetation and water allowed to express themselves. Much as the French people were, nature at Versailles is captive to the will of Louis XIV. He would, no doubt, be happy to learn that the symbol of his power continues to attract and inspire twentieth-century visitors.

With the fabled success of Versailles, the geometric style of landscaping became fashionable throughout much of Europe. It was brought to England in 1660 by Charles II, who, when he returned from exile in the French court, replaced traditional gardens and held sway for the next twenty years. English royal plantsmen were sent to France to study the designs popularized by Le Notre and his followers. Soon parterres, walks, canals, topiary, and statuary flourished on extensive estates and were squeezed onto the smaller grounds of less wealthy but equally pretentious landowners.

Then came the great commercial voyages of the late seventeenth century. English explorers began collecting and shipping home unknown trees and shrubs discovered in Asia and the New World, piquing great excitement and inspiring a surge of horticultural development. The Society of Gardeners, predecessor of the Royal Horticultural Society, was formed in response to this burgeoning fascination with exotic flora. Because few plants were suited to the precise and often tortuous pruning of the Le Notre style, however, the love affair with French design began to fade.

During the eighteenth century, English tourists discovered Italy and were entranced by the rustic Roman campagna. Captured in paintings of Caspar and Nicolas Poussin and Claude Lorraine, which portrayed an idyllic countryside filled with temples and ruins, the Italian landscape became the new passion. Returning English travelers adorned their walls with many of the popular paintings. Such were the forces that inspired a landscape movement that turned away from formal geometry toward a more picturesque concept of nature. Finding fertile soil in England's long tradition of pride in the land, proponents of the new vision sought to idealize their native countryside.

Two figures bear principal responsibility for changing the English concept of gardens: Lancelot "Capability" Brown (1715–83) and Humphrey Repton (1752–1818). Capability Brown reshaped the landscape to fulfill his romantic temperament. Great formal gardens were plowed under to create sinuous hills and valleys, curving paths, and lakes with undulating shorelines. Trees were encouraged to achieve their towering natural shapes, planted singly or in clusters. Humphrey Repton continued this style, replacing formality with a meandering, open aspect. The English landscape was transformed into the lush, gently rolling countryside that continues to be treasured.

URBAN GREEN

Green nature in contemporary urban settings bears some analogy to that at Versailles, being planted within the strict geometric grids of streets and buildings. Although not designed by Le Notre, the city, too, expresses the power of a culture in which vegetation assumes a subservient role, much as do the people who live, work, and play within its steel and glass canyons. The trees, shrubs, lawns, and flowers that decorate metropolitan centers may be considered as elements of a garden constrained by its urban matrix.

Industrialized cities are of relatively recent origin, and the history of their parks and plantings is fairly well known. In the United States, ornamental plants were initially available only for decorating private gardens or small parks and squares. Then, during the mid-nineteenth century, a social view of the role of vegetation began to evolve that was informed by the vision of such urban planners as Frederick Law Olmsted.

Disturbed by the unhealthy condition of families living in cramped tenements, where every breath was fouled with smoke from burning coal,

Olmsted proposed a new role for vegetation to use its ability to relieve the stress of city life. He anticipated the intense growth of metropolitan areas and recognized that human benefit would accrue from setting aside land to remain forever green. Parks would be "lungs" for cities, places for social concourse, where people could relax and breathe air that had been cleansed and refreshed by trees.

Olmsted strongly believed in the restorative quality of green nature. "Scenery," he declared, "worked by an unconscious process to produce relaxing and 'unbending' of faculties made tense by the strain, noise and artificial surroundings of urban life."[3] He reported on the observation of a physician that "a marked improvement in health and vigor has occurred which is to be directly traced to the influence of the park . . . the park has added years to the lives of many of the most valued citizens, and many have remarked that it has much increased their working capacity."[4]

Parks and tree-lined boulevards, Olmsted theorized, would produce strong social benefits by bringing disparate cultural groups together in a healing environment. "He believed that nature had a good effect on the psyche and behavior of man. This moral influence . . . was especially necessary where dwellings crowded together in large cities produced 'morbid conditions of body and mind,' and caused 'nervous feebleness or irritability, and various functional derangements.' By bringing members of the industrialized society into contact with nature and each other in a carefully planned environment, he felt he could increase their aesthetic sensitivity, their physical well-being, and their civilized appreciation of others."[5]

Olmsted's great parks in such metropolitan centers as New York, Boston, and Chicago were instantly successful. People flocked to them to escape the intense pressure of city life. Although the parks fell into some disrepair after World War II, now, after a generation of neglect, his ideas on the benefits of urban green spaces are being confirmed by psychologists and geographers, and his parks are being restored and cherished across the country.

In high-density areas a renaissance of interest in—and an awareness of—the importance of urban vegetation is occurring. Unfortunately, great plots of open space, such as the ones that formed the vast public greens of the nineteenth century, are no longer available. Instead, we are thankful for vest-pocket parks dotted within most major cities—small islands where trees, benches, fountains, and flowers offer respite from the assault of traffic, noise, and pollution. One of the first of these havens, New York

City's Paley Park, is located in the middle of an East Fifty-third Street block on the site of the former Stork Club. Tables and chairs are scattered under the shade of a high canopy of honey locusts. The far wall is obscured by a continuous cascade of water, masking noises from the street. By climbing four steps, pedestrians can easily abandon the bustle of traffic and enter this tranquil, tree-sheltered environment. Here they sit at tables to rest and are soothed by shifting foliage and the gentle murmur of a waterfall.

We go to great effort and expense to bring nature into the city, not only in parks, gardens, and along roadways but also on the sides, roofs, and interiors of buildings. Such integration of plants and buildings continues a very old tradition. Babylon is famed for its hanging gardens, and a palm court, a relic from Victorian times, is still elegantly present in New York's Plaza Hotel.

The modern use of flowers and plants inside buildings was promoted by Macy's Department Store, first in San Francisco and then in New York City. Starting in the 1950s, Macy's stores welcomed each spring with a floral extravaganza. All floors were transformed into bountiful gardens bedecked with arrangements of cut flowers, blooming plants, and potted greenery in an annual event eagerly awaited by hordes of winter-weary customers.

The next phase of integrating plants with structures was initiated in 1963 by the Ford Foundation, which enclosed a living garden within its eleven-story headquarters in New York City. Workers could look down from their offices onto a green oasis. Soon atria became the hallmark of new corporate construction. Plantings featuring large trees and often fountains and ponds appeared in buildings in many metropolitan areas. The IBM Building in New York City boasts a multistoried greenhouse planted with tall clumps of bamboo and furnished with chairs and tables. People seek the area to relax, read, socialize with friends, sip a cup of coffee, and eat lunch. It is an indoor metropolitan park.

Since the 1960s, living plants, led by the ubiquitous *Ficus benjamina*, have become familiar residents inside offices, shopping malls, restaurants, stores, airline terminals, and hospitals. But what is the role of urban vegetation? Why do we care for nature in unnatural surroundings? City plants are much like animals in a zoo. Removed from their native habitat, they are placed in a simulacrum of wilderness, an artificial environment in which they continue life functions under the observation of their human cousins. Yet unlike animals in a zoo, the constant objects of attention, plants in urban surroundings are usually considered as background and temper the hard surfaces of glass, brick, stone, concrete, and macadam.

In addition to its ability to remove pollutants and cool the air through shade and transpiration, urban greenery is important psychologically. It provides a safety valve, giving respite from the constant tension imposed by the built environment. Vegetation allows the human spirit to release itself from the inherent stress of the technosphere and helps it regain stasis and ease. Three settings of green nature are good examples of places that have been specifically designed to influence the visitor's emotional state: the Morton Arboretum in Lisle, Illinois, the Bloedel Reserve at Bainbridge Island, Washington, and Walt Disney World in Lake Buena Vista, Florida.

THE MORTON ARBORETUM

Twenty-six miles west of downtown Chicago, totally surrounded by residential and commercial development, is the green refuge founded by Joy Morton in 1922. It lies in the hilly center of a terminal moraine, on land that had been farmed for fifty years. Morton's dream was to establish an "outdoor museum for the study of woody plants of the world able to support the climate of Illinois, . . . in order to increase the general knowledge and love of trees and shrubs."[6] This was an ambitious undertaking in an area of heavy clay soils and harsh continental climate, where the native vegetation was prairie grassland.

At Morton's insistence, awareness of nature and respect for its wisdom became the hallmark of the institution. The arboretum learned to grow its collections by studying how surviving woody plants had adapted to the stringent midwestern environment, and its display of woody plants from around the globe includes more than 40,300 specimens, which have been tagged and recorded in a computerized catalog. Because Morton directed that the collections be sited carefully to blend with the setting, they are integrated into a flowing naturalistic landscape that provides peace and tranquility for hundreds of thousands of visitors each year.

The arboretum comprises 1,500 acres—natural forests, streams, lakes, collections of trees, shrubs and vines, prairie, fields, lawns, and gardens—all under the huge midwestern sky. Several acres are occupied by roads, parking areas, and buildings that house lecture halls, a library, research laboratories, and offices. Many visitors avail themselves of the rich resources open to them through field trips, classes, lectures, and library privileges, but the vast majority come for a direct outdoor experience of green nature.

The landscape is designed in the English style, characterized by an interplay of two elements: dense tree and shrub areas contrast with open areas of green, carpeted meadow and lawn. Voids are of prime importance, creating separation among groups of trees, defining their boundaries, and providing limits for their flowing masses. As one moves through it, such a landscape continuously invites the eye by the apparent motion of its parts. This is a universal visual phenomenon as, when traveling, closer objects—trees, fences, and power poles—move faster into and out of sight than objects farther away. Thus, in the arboretum landscape, plantings closest to viewers go by more quickly than more distant elements. The seeming migration of clumps of trees planted in open meadows creates an ever-changing composition in which a visitor's passage is translated into a sense of movement within the landscape itself.

As one travels through the arboretum on foot or by car, spaces open, permitting a long view of distant fields, trees, and lakes; then this view becomes obscured while yet another vista opens onto a different setting. The eye is stimulated by the interplay of masses and voids, which permits enticing glimpses but never the whole story at one glance. Such a landscape provides endless interest. Information about the constant opening and closing prospect may be held at a low level of consciousness. Concerns such as where we are going and what lies ahead on the road may overlie the subtle landscape effects. Tony Hiss, an editor at the *New Yorker* and an astute observer, describes "simultaneous perception" as a process by which the mind can free itself from the constraints of linear thinking. Simultaneous perception, he says, allows us to "experience our surroundings and our reactions to them and not just our own thoughts and desires. . . . it lets me gently refocus my attention, and allows a more general awareness of a great many different things at once: sights, sounds, smells, and sensation of touch and balance as well as thoughts and feelings."[7]

The openness of simultaneous perception permits visitors to absorb the totality of their surroundings, including subtle nuances. When people arrive at the Morton Arboretum, their inner beings still reverberating from the stress and tumult of the outside world, a different environment greets them. It is a calm setting, largely excluding signs and symbols of the society outside the gates. They are able to relax and hear the quiet voices of nature as they explore on their own, following paths through fields, plantings, woodland, and prairie where the intellect is less challenged and the spirit is allowed to roam free in serenity.

Visitors become aware of another reality, of nature moving at its own pace. They sense that in some manner what is visible in the landscape is inside themselves as well. Each sight evokes personal feelings that are part of the green experience. Through vistas of woods and fields bright with daffodils, pathways lead to a dam. There, translucent water pours over a curved ledge, boiling where it hits the spillway below and running on to continue the stream whose partial obstruction produced the lake. Visitors are able to transmute the visual quality of the setting into feelings of inner peace.

Throughout the year, the arboretum is an assemblage of instruments whose music, perceived by the eye, echoes deeply within. Springtime is announced early, as willow bark loses its winter brown and softens into shades of yellow. In sheltered places snowdrops bloom—a reassurance that the dark season has passed. Winter honeysuckle pours its delicate lemon scent on the cool air. Trees test the season, sprouting a few tentative green buds. Then, building to a crescendo, trees and shrubs—magnolia, redbud, pear, crab apple, and fragrant viburnum—produce their triumphant spring chorale. Life is renewed.

Weeks before sun-shading leaves appear above, spring's song is played softly on the forest floor, illuminated by light filtering through bare branches. The melody is carried by hepaticas in white, lavender, and blue, red or white trillium, pink clouds of spring beauty, and pale dogtooth violet, whose blooms stand above carpets of speckled leaves. Dutchman's britches snuggle close to tree trunks and spread out in delicate white groupings on shaded slopes. Buds fed by rising sap push through bark, expand, send out pale shoots, and stretch in the sun until mature leaves swivel on their petioles to catch the light. Again they fulfill their ancient mission: transmuting air, moisture, and nutrients into raw materials that plants use for growth, animals for food, and people for the necessities and pleasures of life. In walking through the forest, one becomes a harmonic note in the music.

Summer can be hot and sticky. Mosquitoes whine and stab and fish jump, catching food in midair. A verdant network stretches from soil to treetop. In the gardens, roses, daylilies, and flowering woody plants provide colorful counterpoint for the pervasive chord of green. Prairie extends it roots ever deeper into earth; big bluestem grasses stretch higher than a person to reenact the original drama of the Midwest.

Late August sounds notes that foretell change. Light falls from a different angle. Leaves close down their food production, preparing to separate from branches and return their remaining energy to the earth. Overhead a cacophony of color—first announced by scarlet in the twisted woodbine, followed by orange, yellow, and purple-green—proclaims the approaching end of summer. In the maple forest there comes a magic moment when gold is everywhere; in trees and on the ground, the air vibrates with richness. Then the leaves fall, covering earth with tarnished splendor and leaving black skeletons against the cobalt sky.

Framed by dark conifers, the winter landscape takes on muted tones of brown, black, and gray—subtle colors for the discriminating eye to apprehend. With frosts and gray light winter descends. Almost all is peaceful, but tracks in the snow tell stories of other life that does not cease activity, even in this quiet season.

This is the play of nature at the arboretum, available to visitors as time packages that can be bound into a single day. Long natural rhythms and changes become stratified, staccato pulses under the stroboscopic limit of an individual visit. However, each, by implication, includes all. Nature shares everything with those who care to learn, intimating the diversity and continuity of life.

The arboretum has begun to realize the significance of the restorative quality of its landscape. In a modest research effort, psychologists, led by Herbert W. Schroeder, an environmental psychologist with the U.S. Forest Service, have interviewed members and volunteers to learn more about their responses to it. People were asked to express preference for photographs of distinctive arboretum sites and then discuss the thoughts, feelings, and memories associated with their favorite landscapes. For this group of participants, volunteers, and guides, people very familiar with the arboretum and its values, naturalness of the scene was deemed most important. "Woods," the most highly preferred setting, included views within dense natural forests or views in which natural appearing trees and shrubs predominate. Least-favored scenes included formal landscapes with pruned shrubs and mowed lawns. Of course, preferences might be different for those less familiar with the institution and its emphasis on nature.

Participants in Schroeder's study eloquently revealed their feelings.[8] For some, the arboretum reflects religious values: "Trees towering over the

Morton Arboretum, the spruce tree plot bathed in morning mist. (Courtesy of Morton Arboretum)

road like a cathedral" and "being in the woods is a place where your spirit can fly free, without interruption, bringing you closer to God." For others, the landscape creates a sense of well-being: "A feeling of quiet, peace, and order arises within me"; "majestic, measured, rhythmic beauty"; and "a pleasant tranquil place to be—rather like a living piece of artwork in its impact. It appears orderly, in balance and inviting." Escape from daily routine was also appreciated: "A place of beauty, peace, quiet excitement and refuge from the noise, turmoil, pollution and unpleasantness of traffic and crowded work and living conditions"; "a forest represents to me a cool, calm place to regain composure"; "I think of this as a place to contemplate, to stop and use my senses, to remove myself from today's schedule of events"; and "the arboretum has been a resource and refuge for me through what were often some difficult times." The changing, dynamic character of the landscape over time was important, too: "Perhaps it is comforting to see these flowers blooming again despite whatever else has happened in the world and/or how severe the winter has been." The arboretum evokes wonder: "Very dark and mysterious. Exciting and beautiful. You're surrounded by shadows looking up out at the huge deep open sky"; "there is at once strength and form in these native trees that create a potent force and magic in the area"; and "when the sugar maples are a golden glow, it is magical." Still others enjoyed coming face to face with forces not under human control: "I like to 'touch base' with wildness"; "where forces other than man determine the consequences"; and "the early spring flowers are an especially welcome reminder of the gentler— though indomitable—forces of nature."

To provide a refuge of serenity in an urbanized metropolitan area is to cradle life. Perhaps this is the arboretum's most important role.

THE BLOEDEL RESERVE

On Bainbridge Island, west of Seattle, concern for the visitor's experience has produced another landscape that blends natural and designed settings. In a matrix of old cut-over forest with brooding, second growth of Douglas fir, hemlock, and western red cedar, a series of gardens has been created whose objective is to help guests become aware of their inner feelings about green nature. "The [Bloedel] Reserve's primary interest is in the relationship between plants and people . . . [it is] a place in which to enjoy and learn from the emotional and aesthetic experience of nature the values of harmony, respect for life and tranquility."[9]

The reserve and its philosophical purpose are the legacy of two people, Prentice and Virginia Bloedel, who purchased the property in 1950 as a location for their residence. In the course of establishing their home, Agate Point Farm, and exploring its sixty-seven acres, they discovered that the property's fields and forest held deeply personal meanings for them. The insights they had gained into nature and their relationships with it inspired the Bloedels to create the reserve in 1988. Their goal in setting aside the land was to offer others "the opportunity to enjoy plants both as arranged by man and as they arrange themselves; and for the purpose of providing people wandering about the Reserve a refreshing experience of nature and a broadening of their appreciation of their world. In sum, the Reserve is primarily a place where people may enjoy and learn from the emotional and aesthetic experiences of nature."[10]

Vision, smell, touch, and hearing are fundamental to a visitor's experience of the reserve. Although it includes many fine botanical specimens, none have identifying labels. The founders felt that reading and processing such information might distract from the pure sensory appreciation that was their prime concern. As one walks through the gardens and wild areas, vistas change constantly, revealing visual experiences that resound within the psyche. A series of "rooms" unfolds—a Japanese garden, woodland trail, rhododendron glen, moss garden, reflection pool, and bird refuge, then lakes, streams, and an overlook of Puget Sound. Each encourages visitors to look inward and reflect on the emotions engendered by what is seen. A sense of rightness and harmony prevails. One becomes aware of the presence of a larger order, a realization that "man is not set apart from the rest of nature, he is just a member of that incredibly diverse population of the universe, a member that nature can do without, but that cannot do without nature."[11] Throughout, the reserve is a careful balance of natural and created landscape. This counterpoint is epitomized by the house—handsome and formal in the eighteenth-century French tradition—and its setting in a wild, cut-over forest of towering conifers.

The nearby gardens and woodland walkways artfully blend the natural and the built landscape. Paths lead across the bluff overlooking Puget Sound to a series of woodland trails, past stream and waterfall, and through a rhododendron glen augmented with perennials, wildflowers, and bulbs so artfully planned that nature seems to be the sole designer. The trail emerges upward from a dark woodland to an area meant to encourage private reflection. From the guest house, a subtle blend of Japanese sensibility and Pacific northwestern materials, a rock and sand garden is set against a background of green hillocks—symbolic mountains. Below the house and visible from the deck, a meticulously planted Japanese garden connects a chain of small lakes. The Bloedels identified with the spiritual philosophy that informs Japanese landscape, expressed here in a sense of the harmonious relationship of all life within nature.

One of the great features of the reserve is the reflection pool designed by Thomas Church and surrounded by a wall of yew added by Richard Haag, a landscape architect. Evergreens tower over the hedge, reminders of the forest in which it is placed. Measuring two hundred feet by thirty feet, the simple pool is unadorned except for several curved wooden benches along its sides. Visitors enter the area through an opening in the hedge and can stand and gaze down the pool's length. The side walls of yews direct one's eye to the far end, where it meets a perpendicular wall of green. The lack of a focal point encourages inward contemplation. This green room, with its floor of still water, creates a mystical setting that never fails to soothe the spirit.

All planted areas have been designed to complement and blend with the wild, natural forest, whose floor is dense with ferns and other woodland species. A soft brown path of evergreen needles and bark chips leads to the heart of the reserve. Filtered light discloses great stumps of logged Douglas firs that often serve as nesting places for new plants. Seeds germinate in the rich fecundity of the sheltering forest, sending down roots from their stunted perch to the waiting soil below. If established before the nurse stump disintegrates, the new plants seem to stand on short stilts. However, should the stump disintegrate before they can fully establish themselves, the saplings will often be blown over in a storm. They will usually survive and, in time, resume their vertical growth, leaving a small grove to mark the site of the vanished stump.

Fallen logs of Douglas fir and red cedar may also nurture new plants. Most commonly, western hemlock, Douglas fir, evergreen or red huckleberry, salal, cascara, lady fern, and salmonberry will grow on the log or in its shelter. Years later, after the nurse log has rotted, it is memorialized by the trees and shrubs it sheltered. Similarly, one can find colonies of polypody fern growing where a fallen big-leaf maple had lain, leaving behind the ferns that had decorated its bark while it lived. The rich old forest sings its song of life's renewal for all who wish to hear. This is the landscape that spoke so eloquently to the Bloedels. "We found single plants and colonies of fragile woodland species, mosses, ferns, a world of incomparable diversity, a panorama of survival in the eternal struggle, exciting in its vitality," the Bloedels remembered. "We found that plants often have a way of arranging and disposing themselves with a harmony of color, texture and form when left to themselves. We discovered that there is a grandeur in decay; the rotten log hosting seedlings of hemlocks, cedars, huckleberries, the shape of a crumbling snag."[12]

The essence of the reserve is to be found in the way that visual settings echo in the minds and spirits of those who view it. "It is intended [that] the Reserve be a place where visitors find beauty and tranquility; one that captures the magic and mystery of nature and breaks the connection with the outside world."[13] Intuitively the Bloedels understood the relationship between people and green nature, sensing that it could lead to an awakening of the human spirit and foster respect, stewardship, and conservation. In peaceful contemplation, the Bloedel Reserve presents an experience designed to bring visitors face to face with deeper issues, the role of humans as part of nature. In many years of studying people-plant interactions, I have found no other place created for this specific purpose.

Seeds of the western hemlock germinate and grow on stumps of logged Douglas fir, sending roots down to the soil below. (Courtesy of Mary Randlett)

Walt Disney World

Each year millions of visitors enter the Magic Kingdom near Orlando, Florida, to be enchanted and entertained. Troubles disappear in the Magic Kingdom, where visitors are greeted by Mickey Mouse himself, his face shining from a huge tapestry stitched in plants. Each day of the year more than three thousand begonias, alternanthera, pansies, or alyssum create a visual welcome. Color seems to vibrate from architecture, flags, vegetation, and the costumes of the Disney characters. Castles, Old World–style buildings, futuristic constructions, a haunted Victorian mansion, and the scaled-down Crystal Palace are all set in a bouquet of flowers, shrubs, trees, lawns, and fountains.

Plantings are everywhere. Beds swirl in intricate floral patterns and sit like jewels in emerald lawns. At eye level, hanging baskets, cascades of living color, festoon lamp posts and trees. Green topiary creatures cavort: Elephants balance on balls and lead each other in line. They are joined by a convoluted sea serpent, dancing hippos, ducks, Snow White and her seven companions, and even Mary Poppins—complete with umbrella. Each plant delivers a positive subliminal message, providing the lift meant to guarantee enjoyment of this fantasy land.

Throughout the resort, plants help create specific geographic settings. At Big Thunder Mountain Railroad, a southwestern desert landscape features spineless yucca, Texas ebony, mesquite, barrel cactus, prickly pear, jumping cholla, and saguaro cactus. Tom Sawyer Island in the Mississippi basin is evoked through look-alike plants and natives of that area: Tall maples, sweet gum, oaks, pines, and sycamores create the green background for outcroppings of fern and orange pyracantha. Weeping willows are mirrored at the water's edge. The Jungle Cruise ride takes visitors through dense tropical vegetation highlighted with bamboo, giant philodendron, flowering orchids, bromeliads, shell ginger, and other exotics, among which lurk such lifelike "inhabitants" as crocodiles, native hunters, and elephants, all of whom appear on cue.

Landscaping tells stories and defines settings. At Mickey's Starland, subtle shifts in scale create a cartoonlike ambience. All structures—Mickey's house and farm buildings (with real goats on the roof)—are realized in a distorted scale, creating a child-sized world. Plants are part of the gentle conspiracy. Growing in oversized window boxes on Mickey's undersized house, dwarf hibiscus flaunt huge, red flowers. In a similar deceit, large, rainbow-bright gerbera daisies substitute for smaller white field

At Walt Disney World, a topiary Mary Poppins welcomes visitors. (© The Walt Disney Company)

daisies along a fence. Ground beds feature great convoluted heads of cockscomb that resemble pastel brains borne on dwarf plants, so fantastic they must be touched to be believed by young visitors.

Tucked in a corner is Granny Duck's Farm, a small-scale reproduction where full-size corn, peppers, eggplant, pumpkins, and sunflowers grow. It is a revelation for those youngsters who think vegetables are made in the supermarket. A maze with green walls of fig (_Ficus repens_) topped with bright flowers that change with the seasons is a favorite spot. Strategically placed within the maze are "poof" fountains, balls of mist that appear magically for one second in an irregularly timed pattern.

Tomorrowland is articulated by its futuristic design of flower beds, palms, and other trees, all helping to create a high-tech look. Palms have a natural architectural growth, but other trees are sheared into geometric forms. Planter boxes coax flowering plant material into structural shapes that reflect the contemporary colors and sharp lines of the surrounding architecture.

In World Showcase at Epcot, plants are carefully selected to reflect the locale of each international experience. The landscape of the Canada showcase uses look-alike flora that is comfortable in Florida but appears to be northern. Himalayan deodar cedar and Chinese junipers replace the firs and spruce that would not survive a subtropical climate. The gardens of the Morocco showcase emphasize the agricultural importance of a country at the edge of the Sahara Desert. Date palms and citrus, olive, pomegranate, loquat, and banana trees are underlain with beds of peppermint, basil, and seasonal vegetable crops. Walkways connecting the international showcases are lined with green camphor trees, giving visual unity to the diverse pavilions and gardens.

Throughout, the flower show takes its cue from Katy Moss Warner, director, parks horticulture, who has gained a special sensitivity to the ways that plants "speak" to visitors. "Screamers" announce themselves, shouting, "Hey, look at me!" "Wow!" plants include both topiary creatures and brilliantly colored flowers that hail guests from strategically placed beds. "Talkers" speak gently. Manicured, weed-free lawns, large shade trees, and plants of varying tones and textures of green throughout the parks all say, "Welcome. Isn't this pleasant? Please enjoy your stay."

"Whisperers" communicate primarily with the botanically or horticulturally astute. Through subtle qualities—unusual form, bark, or leaves—whisperers invite detailed inspection, "Look at me closely, I'm different, I have features you may have never seen before." Both whisperer and screamer are combined in bright hanging baskets suspended from lamp posts. Baskets lift gardens into the air and provide color for all—especially on days when visiting throngs obscure the patterns of the ground beds. The horticultural feat of using hanging baskets to raise color into the air is, of itself, a whisper, although basket plants selected for bold display color combinations are screamers, demanding attention.

Sounds and scents can be whisperers, too. At the Moroccan showcase, beds of mint and basil are lightly bruised each morning to release their fragrance. Katy Moss Warner considers displays focused on geographic authenticity and species conservation as whisperers. "People come to enjoy the screamers and talkers," she observes, "but are delighted when they come upon a rare or endangered plant and its label, which whispers to them that diversity in the plant kingdom is important, too."

The gardens of Walt Disney World provide experiences in which plants fulfill specific functions. The superb maintenance of all vegetation and the cleanliness of the facilities might be considered as a whisper, giving a message of quality. Visitors respond by elevating their own behavior.

Vandalism is a rarity in these beautifully maintained parks. As performers, plants must appear "on stage" at the correct moment. In December, ten thousand chrysanthemums in beds, baskets, and cascades disappear overnight, and gardeners work around the clock to replace them with ten thousand poinsettias. At next day's opening, the entire kingdom proclaims the Christmas season.

One theme that threads through these three attractions is a visitor's experience. For most people, being in nature awakens feelings that remain internalized, rarely brought to conscious awareness. Still, somewhere below intellect flickers a shimmer of feeling about what is seen. We function on at least two levels: In one, thoughts result from a conscious reasoning effort, as when we solve a problem; the other is the unconscious knowing that has evolved in humans along with our more elegant intellectual processes.

Delineating this has long been the search of many disciplines—philosophy, psychology, religion, medicine, and art. Each provides a window on that "unknown knower": soul, spirit, intuition, and reflex are some of the postulates for responses that lie within. Exploring the subtle relationships between green nature and human nature can provide yet another portal through which we can view and learn to understand our complex selves and become aware of the hidden sources of knowledge we use daily.

ANOTHER WAY OF KNOWING

I have referred many times to experiences with nature that are not the result of conscious thought. "My heart leaps up" is the recurring example. When the emotional component is strong—fear, fright, or joy—we are well aware of its presence. At other times it is subtle and more difficult to identify—the sense of well-being that can result from time spent out of doors, perhaps walking in the woods. This sense is not intellectual. It is a distinct feeling, but one which, unless we really are paying attention, is likely to pass unconsidered. The important point is that it is noncognitive. We do not think first and then experience the feeling. It just happens. In a similar but less emotional way, we respond inwardly to landscapes, consistently preferring the open woods, paths curving out of sight, or scenes with a partially obstructed view. Participants in the landscape preference studies discussed earlier cannot say how they made their choices; they made them instinctively. This intuition is at work in everyone at all times.

How do we know what we know? We can add pieces of information and come to a conclusion through inductive reasoning. We can figure out that it might be dangerous to walk under a ladder, particularly if someone is standing on it, painting a wall (deductive reasoning). Or, we can come to know intuitively. A rainbow or a beautiful view might do it for us.

In this chapter I have tried to describe the kinds of experiences that occur through observation of nature. However such descriptions can never be more than a pale approximation of the event. It is like eating chocolate ice cream. One could describe the creamy, smooth texture on the tongue, the cool melting in the mouth, and the taste that remains after the last swallow. But description does not satisfy. The only way to know chocolate ice cream is to eat some. Once having had it, you can recall all its subtleties in a way that no verbal description can duplicate. So it is with experiencing a preferred landscape. Although not quite as simple as purchasing a chocolate ice cream cone, we can become aware of our responses to such settings: Bodily response provides the clue.

Our home on the grounds of Morton Arboretum was walled with large glass windows that overlooked a lake. The view was southerly and, particularly during the summer, there was a strong buildup of heat due to the sun. I requested that a tree be planted in front of the living-dining room windows to try to reduce the insolation, although I was concerned that it would adversely affect our view of the lake. The tree was planted.

We then had to look through its branches to see the water and were surprised to discover that, far from detracting from the view, the tree somehow enhanced it.

This unexpected development aroused my curiosity, leading me to experiment as I walked through the arboretum. I chose a series of sites, first peering from behind a tree, then moving aside to see the unobstructed view. (I must have looked rather peculiar while doing this.) I soon noticed that the change of position brought with it a very subtle, almost visceral, shift within me. Somehow I could actually *feel* the difference in the views. I learned to become aware of the feeling associated with landscape settings and began to watch for it. Once recognized, I could discern that inner tug frequently; it happened almost all the time as I walked through the arboretum, but at so subjective a level that I was only aware of it if I really "listened" with the center of my body. This type of revelation is surely what is meant by the expression "gut feeling."

The arboretum's staff artist Nancy Stieber invited me to speak with her watercolor class about experiencing the landscape. Some of her students were finding it difficult to choose a specific subject to paint, moving from place to place until they finally found a satisfactory setting. Rather than intellectualizing their decision, I wondered whether the artists might learn to listen to their inner selves and let their gut feelings tell them what to paint. It was a challenge to see if I could help others become aware of the sensation I had recently discovered.

To introduce the session, I told them that we would take a short walk and try to turn off the "thinker" within us and give free rein to the "experiencer." Our first stop was under a low-branched spreading hawthorn at the edge of a large meadow. I asked the class to stand by the tree trunk, under its green canopy, and slowly walk out into the open, trying to detect a shift of feeling within themselves as they moved from beneath the tree into the field. It took about four attempts before they could actually pinpoint the change. Next, we repeated the exercise, starting under a high-branched elm. We noted how different it felt to be under that tree's vaulting arch rather than the low-branched hawthorn, then walked into the open field to experience our response to that change of space.

Class was held at Thornhill, a one-story stone structure at the top of a sloping, woods-encircled lawn. We began our walk at one side, where a planting of trees and shrubs partially obstructed the building. Then, as we moved into the field, its full facade was exposed. I asked the students to decide which views they most enjoyed. They were amazed to discover that they preferred those in which Thornhill was partially obscured by vegetation, describing them as being more mysterious.

We continued to sample different areas, walking into a small forest and noting the difference in feeling as we entered or left. We stood on a curving path that led down toward a wooded area while its other segment led straight up the hill toward the building. Which did they like better? Most spontaneously chose the curving path. I included several more sites that would have rated high on preference studies, and each time the students voted with their gut feeling. By the end of our time together, they were convinced that it was indeed possible to become aware of one's intuitive, physical responses to landscape settings.

At the end of the week-long class, Nancy Stieber disclosed the effect of our session. Where before the session artists had often spent days intellectualizing their search for the "right" scene, afterward they were quickly able to select their subject by listening to their senses, and the finished work expressed a deeper appreciation of the setting.

I believe this demonstrates the right brain-left brain phenomenon. The left brain organizes sensory information in a cognitive manner, whereas the right brain is creative and experiences it directly. The exercises we did helped teach us to think with the right side of the brain. I have repeated them in a number of classes and consistently find that, after minimal practice, most people are able to "hear" their gut feeling.

Herbert Schroeder provided new insight to those arboretum classes.[14] The kind of "body experience" that we were learning to recognize had been discussed by Eugene Gedlin, a psychologist at the University of Chicago, who called it a "felt sense." He described it as "not a mental experience but a physical one. A body awareness of a situation or person or event. An internal aura that encompasses everything you feel and know about the given subject at a given time—encompasses it and communicates it to you all at once rather than detail by detail. Think of it as a taste, if you like, or great musical chord that makes you feel a powerful impact, a big round unclear feeling."[15] Gedlin used the felt response as part of his technique of focusing, used in psychotherapy.

One does not actually have to be in the setting, Schroeder suggests: "You might be able to sense [that] change by simply imagining yourself in a deep silent forest and then in an open sunny meadow. . . . Better yet look at some pictures of different kinds of outdoor environments, or actually go to a place where you can walk back and forth between a place enclosed by trees and a place open to the sky."[16]

The important thing is to listen to the inner self. Do not analyze what you are doing, and after a bit of practice you will find your felt sense. Once you recognize it, try it out on different settings. View a building through trees, then straight on; compare an unobstructed view of a mountain with one seen through the branches of a tree. The felt sense is somewhat similar to Tony Hiss's simultaneous perception. In *Experience of Place* he describes the effects of simultaneous perception as he traverses Prospect Park in Brooklyn, New York. I have walked that path with Tony Hiss's description in hand as a guidebook, and highly recommend it as another way of becoming familiar with the subjective feelings through which we experience our surroundings.

Although our subjective feelings delineate green nature as experience, when economic uses are discovered for its various components green nature becomes a resource. As such it is manipulated and exploited for monetary gain or the "good of society." This view leads along a dangerous course that satisfies society's immediate wants but ignores the long-term price of human actions.

> Manipulation of the natural environment for human benefit is necessary and appropriate to a point. But if this attitude is carried too far we lose our awareness of what it means to be in a non-manipulative relationship with nature. . . . When we are unable or unwilling to take delight in natural things that are not under our control, we become domineering and manipulative toward our environment, caring only about benefits that can be justified in scientific and economic terms. Our economic calculations then lead us to replace trees and forest with roads, parking lots, and buildings. We pay a heavy price in terms of increased stress, alienation from our environment, and inability to relate to anything outside our narrow egocentric goals. We continue to pay this price because so many of us are unaware of what we are losing.[17]

Neil Evernden is an environmental philosopher who uses the concept of space to draw distinctions between physical and human values. "Space is neutral and measurable, easily contained on maps," he observes. "Place is unmeasurable because it depends on the involvement of an individual and exists only within him. Place, like beauty, is detectable only through a living person."[18] He helps us to see the fallacy in the resource view of nature, which Paul Sheppard called "the most insidious form of nature hating because it poses as virtue, as prudent, foreseeing, and unselfish. It destroys the world and ourselves in spite of the altruism of its protagonists."[19]

We intuitively identify green nature as experience, not resource. We do not need to dominate and manipulate nature, but should rather participate with it to achieve society's cultural and economic goals.

4

Participation with Green Nature: Gardening

I love the smell of the dirt, the smell of the grass, I love to plant, to watch anything that grows. I kneel down and take up a handful of dirt and say: this is nature, this is God's thing.

—Victor Pomare, community gardener, Roxbury, Boston, Massachusetts

The previous chapter considered how we, as observers of green nature, might be affected by seeing, smelling, and perhaps touching it. How might the responses change if we become personally involved with creating the living green? What might be felt when we sow seeds and nurture the plants from appearance of first tentative leaves until they mature, bloom, or bear fruit? Our participation through physical and mental investment draws us into a deeper level of experience, creating a closer person-plant relationship than occurs for passive observers. The most intimate person-plant relationship occurs in gardening, where we physically participate in maintaining green nature. We water and fertilize, pinch and stake, and note the color and size of leaves to determine the success of our care.

We have been taught to understand the world in terms of subject and object. What we are trying to envision in people-plant interactions is a unity, person and plant joined together, the human experience of a non-human object. Think of what happened to Alice when she stepped through the looking glass: familiar things came alive in a different context. A deck of cards turned into people, flamingos were transformed into mallets, and hedgehogs became balls in a fantastic game of croquet. So, too, if we step through the looking glass that separates people from plants and let personal responses be our guide, we will find ourselves in a new world where human experience creates an unexpected dimension. It becomes the connecting link of an interacting system joining green nature and human nature.

PHYSICAL AND MENTAL GARDENS

When considering gardens and gardening we recognize two images. The first is the physical garden, the familiar flowers, trees, and shrubs of a three-dimensional world. The second is the mental garden that is found "through the looking glass"—nonphysical, seldom perceived, and occurring in the infinite dimensions of the mind. The two are joined by an experience that results from their interaction.

If asked what gardening is about, we would quickly answer, "Plants." Watered, fertilized, pinched, potted, pampered, cursed, and loved—the plant reigns supreme. A plant-centered view of gardening is incomplete, however. Anyone who has ever potted a geranium, tended a fragrant flower border, or weeded a vegetable plot knows that more is involved. Consider: for whose benefit are garden books written and plant societies and garden clubs established? Were Latin names invented so plants would know who *they* are, or so people could communicate with each other about specific plants?

Species are sought, discovered, propagated, bred, bought, and sold to satisfy the interests of people. Horticulture and gardening are human constructs, umbrellas to accommodate anyone bitten by the plant bug. Plants do not need people, but people do indeed need plants. If flowers, gardens, and all of green nature are to be understood from a human perspective, the varieties of feelings they generate within us must be taken into account. A plant can be considered an object that has physical and chemical attributes, an arrangement of matter appearing in a particular guise. The luminous pink zinnia in the garden comprises molecules organized into leaves, stems, and flowers that perform life functions. It is a biological entity and can be no more than that until someone sees it. Then—eureka!—atoms, leaves, stems, and flowers are suffused with personal meanings. No longer a singular, three-dimensional object, the zinnia is transmuted into a concept, a stimulus for thoughts and feelings.

In its conceptual translation, this zinnia can become a beacon of hope or a means of getting to know the neighbors. Such transformation of botany into humanity occurs continuously in mental gardens, and once we become adept at stepping through the looking glass we can begin to understand their importance in daily life.

In ancient days, the earth's journey from winter through spring to summer solstice was calculated by positions of the sun. Early calendars marked the dates for rituals and ceremonies that alerted the populace to prepare for the planting season soon to come. Now, although we do not have specific rites to remind us of spring's approach, an annual phenomenon alerts gardeners to spring's advent while the earth is still locked in wintry cold. It causes hearts to beat faster and initiates an endless chain of mental preparation. This phenomenon is the arrival of seed catalogs, whose promised bounties are an antidote for frozen soil, monotonous landscapes, and lack of sunlight. Photos of brilliant flowers or perfect fruits and vegetables stimulate something in our brains, and we embark on a journey that will last for months—planning, planting, and caring for a garden. In a green euphoria, we anticipate the pleasures to be. The heady explosion overwhelms memories of sweating under the glaring sun, digging and pulling thistles, trapping voracious slugs, or staking sagging stems. All is glorious as we cultivate our mental garden.

Like a lover's kiss, gardening is almost as much to be enjoyed in the anticipation as in the actual act. Days of poring over catalogs heighten expectations of splendor that lies ahead. Possibly more gardening activity occurs in the imagination than in the confines of a garden plot. We know the touch and smell of soil, seeds, plants, flowers, vegetables, and fruits, but what is understood about their mental counterpart—the river of thoughts and feelings that begins as a mere trickle with the idea that we might want to make a garden this year?

As the planting season approaches, that pleasant, meandering stream turns into a swift current that drags us heedlessly through the calendar. The best of schedules becomes the hapless victim of torrential rains when soil should be tilled, of cold when seeds should be sprouting, and of unseen critters lurking in the shadows, ready to decapitate tender shoots or carve hideous designs in lush, healthy leaves. In the midst of the rush are small, quiet eddies, where we pause to marvel at the transformation of brown seeds into tender shoots of pale jade. At last, sometime during midsummer, the stream regains its calm aspect, shrinking back within its banks. We can relax and savor the results of our ride through the rapids.

The tumultuous pleasure of this annual trip occurs in our brain where are planted all the meanings associated with gardening: feelings of nurturing, pride of creating something new and alive, and the comfort of being in partnership with nature. Thus, in order to understand the human aspects of this activity, we must acknowledge that our mental garden is as real as its physical counterpart. The mental garden can be a reservoir of hidden feelings or a source of inspiration. Moments come for which we are unprepared. Suddenly, the scent of lilacs, the glimpse of a seedling breaking through soil, or the sound of water overwhelm us. The experience occurs in a flash; only afterward do we stop to analyze our reaction. Feelings that precede thought emanate from someplace other than the manipulating cognitive senses.

These responses are difficult to capture, identify, and analyze. We accept them simply as transient sparks of emotion that do not interrupt the patterns of daily life, ignoring what might be an important source of self-knowledge. Such inspired moments could open an avenue for exploration and appreciation of an important aspect of our inner selves.

The Process of Gardening

The human meanings may, perhaps, become more evident if we consider gardening as a process, a series of actions that produce visible products: flowers, vegetables, trees, shrubs, or lawns. To go through the looking glass and move beyond plants is to find what gardeners experience while growing them. The process begins even before a seed is entrusted to soil. It is initiated with that first glimmer—"Perhaps I will make a garden"—and continues through all subsequent thoughts, actions, and responses (perspiration, exasperation, and, sometimes, exultation) that occur from sowing seeds to the flowering of the mature plant.

Most easily grasped are the ideas that race through our minds as we plan the garden. We debate its site and size, which plants to grow and how they will be arranged, and which cultivars we will allow to bloom in our treasured kingdom. Such ideas might be considered as byproducts, mental events that occur as we raise our cherished peonies and cucumbers. The difference between gardening as an activity and gardening as psychological experience is the difference between what the gardener does and what the gardener feels. We must gain a new perspective that will allow us to step back and observe ourselves as gardeners who observe and respond to green nature.

When gardening is considered as a partnership of person and plant, a symbiotic relationship that benefits both organisms, its human importance becomes apparent. This special vantage point gives entry to the wonderland we create within ourselves wherein we sow and cultivate all the nuances of the gardening process. Through it we become aware of the incredible richness to be found in our interaction with plants. Gardening is loved not only for what is produced in the soil but also for the joy with which it rewards each gardener. The world of feelings merits the same careful attention as the enticing catalogs that brighten our January evenings.

PEACE OF MIND

In 1976 the psychologist Rachel Kaplan and I explored the types of pleasure people find in gardening.[1] As part of the American Horticultural Society's People/Plant Program, we sent a two-page questionnaire to society members. Thirty-six statements about the satisfactions of gardening, including horticultural ("trying new kinds of plants, growing odd or unusual plants") and personal ("producing some of my own food, seeing plants grow"), were divided into nine categories. AHS members were asked, "When you think of the satisfaction *you* get from gardening, how important is *each* of these to you?"

We would have considered a thousand replies a good sample, but the questions must have touched a hidden wellspring. AHS members completed and returned 4,297 surveys and even included letters expanding on their answers, describing their emotional responses to their gardens. Their obvious enthusiasm was not restricted to our survey questions. Rachel and Stephen Kaplan have commented, "The significance of gardening was expressed in many ways, some eloquent, some simple, some with sadness in anticipation of moving, and others with a clear mission [e.g., 'Grow garlic!']."[2]

The American Horticultural Society had long brought its members a great variety of information about plants, but the survey opened a new door: human issues in horticulture. Gardeners were eager to share their feelings. Although AHS members have a high degree of knowledge and horticultural sophistication, their top-rated satisfaction was not growing the most beautiful rose or rarest peony. The most beneficial aspect was described as achieving an inner sense of serenity. More than 60 percent of the respondents gave "peacefulness and tranquility" as their most important reward for gardening.

Rachel and Stephen Kaplan also invited readers of *Organic Gardening and Farming* to participate in the survey. That group "tended to be

younger, distinctively less affluent, and more oriented to growing vegetables than the AHS participants."[3] Yet those surveyed rated peacefulness
and quiet even more highly than did the AHS members. The ability of
gardening to enhance psychological well-being was common to both
groups, something we found expressed time after time as we examined
gardening in a wide range of settings.

GROWING SELF-ESTEEM

Where should one begin in trying to find the mental counterpart of
the visible garden, to discern the psychological equivalents of sprouting
seeds, new leaves and stems, opening blossoms, and ripening fruits and
discovering what it really means to make a garden? Just as the gleam of a
candle is more visible in a dimly lighted room, so the human benefits of
gardening are more clearly seen in impoverished environments that lack
the amenities to make life pleasant.

The physical condition of a community, its buildings, streets, and vacant spaces, makes an enormous difference in the way members of that
community feel about themselves. What we see often tells us what we are.
"Walking by and through trash-filled empty lots and vandalized school
yards, walking along littered streets with no trees, seeing only pavement
and brick when looking out the window makes people feel bad about
where they live and about themselves," argue Robert M. Hollister and
Christine Cousineau. "They know they do not matter, that their pleasure
or comfort is unimportant." Lyndon Johnson observed that "ugliness can
demean the people who live among it. What a citizen sees everyday is his
America: if it is attractive, it adds to the quality of his life, if it is ugly it
can demean his existence."[4] The physical condition of a community, therefore, plays a double role. For the community, it is a measure of itself; for
outsiders, it creates an impression of community quality and character.

In the anguish of inner-city ghettos, where life is a constant contest for
survival, surprising gardens can be found in window boxes, back yards,
vacant lots, and on the grounds of public housing projects. It is in harsh
settings such as these that, by contrast, the joy and tranquility of gardening can most easily be seen. My introduction to these human values came
in 1962, when I volunteered to assist the New York City Housing Authority in initiating a garden contest for its residents, a pioneering program
that has inspired many others around the country. The NYCHA, the larg-
est landlord in the world, wanted to encourage some of its seven hundred

thousand tenants to plant gardens on the grounds surrounding the high-rise towers.

For the contest—which still continues—the Authority's responsibilities include organizing the contest, digging up the beds in spring, and providing a stipend for purchasing materials. From then on, tenants are on their own. The gardeners decide on the landscape design and types of vegetation to be used. They plant and maintain the beds through August, when a panel of judges—horticulturists, garden writers, and others—inspects each plot to select winning entries. The program culminates in an honors ceremony in October. Audience excitement is palpable, reaching a cheering climax as color slides of winning gardens are flashed on a screen. Every participant receives a certificate, and the beaming winners are given handsome trophies engraved with their names. After the meeting, almost everyone leaves in a state of exhilaration, determined to carry off one of those prestigious awards the following year.

Gardening in the ghetto has the obvious esthetic benefits of chrysanthemums blooming among sterile high-rises, beauty validating hope in barren neighborhoods. But observing the plantings provides only horticultural or botanical information. How can one discover the gardens that bloom in the spirit? The best way is to talk with the tenants who daily tend their precious plots. As a judge, I did this—inviting them to express their feelings about their creations. Although my initial contacts occurred many years ago, they remain fresh in my memory. There was a shy, dark-eyed woman who had made a garden in front of her high-rise building on Avenue D on Manhattan's Lower East Side. When I asked her why, she replied softly in Spanish-tinged words, "They told me that you couldn't grow flowers on Avenue D, but I wanted to try. Now you should see the old folks come out every day to enjoy the flowers." Indeed, some elderly residents basked on nearby benches, taking pleasure in the garden.

After judging many entries, I began to realize that the very existence of fragile gardens in these devastated neighborhoods was itself something of a miracle. Often unfenced, marigolds, zinnias, and petunias advertised themselves, blooming recklessly in contrast to their scarred surroundings. I wondered how such vulnerable beauty could survive in an area where automobiles and buildings were regularly vandalized. In Spanish Harlem I questioned a policeman about the incredible durability of the plantings. How did they escape destruction? He didn't know, but suggested asking the gardeners themselves. At the next stop I did. A gray-haired man replied, "We know who the trouble-makers are, so we invite them to join our garden group, and assign them the job of guarding it. Now we have no more trouble!" The simplicity and appropriateness of their solution was astonishing.

I asked the same question at other gardens and discovered that each had developed its own protection plan. Most surprising, none called for police assistance. Tenants, wise to the ways of their neighborhoods, took care of the problem in their own way. At one high-rise building, a gardener said, "See those windows up there? People are assigned to them, some with binoculars. They watch over the garden and sound the alarm if anyone messes with it." At another, boys and girls were scheduled for guard duty at certain hours. Often mothers sat by the plantings with their babies. The whole issue was summed up by a woman on the East Side who said she expected no vandalism because "all the rotten kids are *in* the contest this year."

A new vista opened for me at a garden created by a group of teen-aged boys under the guidance of a social worker. It was "Japanese"— brick-edged with carefully laid out pebble paths and a pond, neatly dug and lined with plastic and spanned by a well-constructed wooden bridge. The social worker told us the boys had worked intensely all summer, foraging throughout the debris of Manhattan to return with boards and other necessary construction materials. The boys were obviously proud of their accomplishment. Then the social worker told us that each of them had been in trouble with the law. At that stage of my awareness such a fact was difficult to comprehend. Never, in my naïveté, had I associated gardening with anyone in conflict with society. Now I was shaken by the reality that it could be compatible with having a police record. My provincial view of gardening as a suburban pastime was obviously inadequate and needed expansion. It made me wonder how it was that people in different social settings could derive the same kinds of pleasure from a garden. What qualities of gardening allowed it to transcend cultural and economic circumstances? I gradually realized that the appeal lay not so much in the plants, but rather in the feelings they generated in the gardeners.

The insight revealed a new world to me, one in which the subtle human benefits of gardening perhaps outweighed the esthetic and material value of the flowers and vegetables produced. That meticulous "Japanese" garden and the joyous blossoms on Avenue D propelled me on a continuing search to understand the intimate relationships between plants and the people who nurture them.

For tenants of the housing authority, the gardens become special places, focuses for social activities. Wedding and graduation pictures are taken at the favored sites. One tenant wrote, "What is more important is everyone getting to know each other, everyone smiles and discusses our garden, they worry about too much rain, not enough rain, they're all so pleased that children are interested in caring, not destroying. From early morning to late at night you can see neighbors leaning over the garden fence. It has become the center spot of our court where everyone is a friend."

The gardens produced unexpected benefits; residents who grew flowers and vegetables joined together in a warm kind of pride and neighborliness. They saw to it that the beds and surrounding areas were kept neatly groomed. Paper and trash were removed quickly, and groundsmen were urged to mow adjacent lawns more frequently. Tenants no longer "airmailed garbage," throwing bags filled with refuse out the windows. Vandalism was reduced both outside and inside the buildings. Where it had been common practice to destroy new plantings around public housing, tenants now began requesting permission to help landscape the buildings. Garden clubs have been organized in many of the projects. What happened seems clear: The affirmative experience of gardening helped residents achieve a more positive attitude about themselves as well as about their buildings and grounds.

The changing composition of low-income urban populations was another factor affecting the success of urban gardening programs. During the 1960s, post–World War II migration from South to North was at full flood. New residents of public housing brought with them skills and memories of traditional rural ways, and planting a garden in these strange metropolitan surroundings helped them reestablish connections with their past. This is borne out by their comments and actions. In Chicago, for example, residents of high-rise public housing buildings objected to using "front yard gardens" for raising vegetables. They said, "Grow flowers in front, vegetables belong in the back yard." I met an elderly woman in Manhattan who worked with a group of children to create an unusual garden: everything was planted in rows, each marked with an identifying label. Into this urban garden she had put flowers such as tuberous begonias, along with okra and cotton from her southern childhood. She explained, "It is important for children to know the names of all the plants, even some that they don't see up here." Clearly, she was trying to transmit part of the cultural traditions of her past to connect the youngsters with their own heritage.

The gardening program of the NYCHA has been a model, replicated in cities such as Chicago, Birmingham, Seattle, and Vancouver. Although NYCHA values the program highly for its human benefits and continues to provide solid support, programs in other cities have not always prospered. They can become prey to political forces with an agenda that fails to see the importance of making self-esteem bloom in low-income neighborhoods. In addition to public housing, however, low-income areas can provide other settings where gardens may flourish. Window boxes, planters, and community plots can serve as initial steps toward creating a sense of neighborliness and harmony.

A Philadelphia Story

Gardening's social potential is clearly demonstrated in the pioneering window-box program of Philadelphia's Neighborhood Gardening Association, conceived in 1953 by Louise Bush-Brown, a horticulturist, author, and teacher. Well aware of the city's endless blocks of poverty and degradation, Bush-Brown sought a way for people to help themselves and paired residents of blocks that showed interest in improving their surroundings with suburban garden clubs and church groups that wished to assist them. The Neighborhood Gardening Association was the link.

Residents supplied the impetus for establishing gardens by applying to the Neighborhood Gardening Association for consideration as a "Garden Block." When 80 percent of the families on a block agreed to take care of their plantings for two years, the association assigned a participating garden club to supply all materials and work with them to create the window-box gardens.

From its inception in 1957, Bush-Brown saw the program as more than cosmetic, knowing that it would also be a way of encouraging residents to gain a new sense of community pride and achievement. Her first Garden Block manual reveals hopes that transcend horticulture. "One of the greatest joys of gardening is the happiness which comes from the sharing of one's flowers with others. And a window box offers very special opportunities for this sharing of beauty, for to friends and neighbors and all who pass along the street it gives a lift to the heart just to look at it."[5]

Planter boxes were only the beginning. Once they were in place, residents were inspired to tackle other tasks to improve their surroundings: clearing garbage-littered empty lots, painting and repairing front steps, and building facades. The most eloquent comments about the value of these miniature gardens come from the gardeners themselves: "Nothing, absolutely nothing, could have been done for this block what these flowers have done! For the first time neighbors have learned to work together"; and, "A year ago we didn't even know each other to speak to by name, and now we are all neighbors working together."[6]

Since my first visit to Philadelphia in 1962 to see Louise Bush-Brown and the window boxes, I have returned often to track the progress and expansion of that simple concept. During my initial visit she took me to meet the people responsible for the program. I saw block after block of window boxes, clean streets, and painted houses. Wherever we went, people expressed pride in the wonders that had been accomplished and joy in being part of their restored neighborhoods. Their deep affection for Louise Bush-Brown was obvious in the warm welcome she received everywhere.

Why should petunias blooming in a window box lead to cleaned streets and repaired buildings? Once again the residents provided insight: "Before it was just a house, now it looks like home"; and, "I've lived on this block for fifteen years. It's so nice to come to know the names as well as the faces of the other people on the block. I never knew them before." Next to what had been a debris-filled lot and was now a small garden, the comments were, "This was the most dumpified place I had ever seen. Now it even smells good"; and, "I guess I'll wash my windows now."

More than one hundred blocks continue the window-box tradition as part of Philadelphia Green, a comprehensive program sponsored by the Pennsylvania Horticultural Society. In addition to flower boxes, Philadelphia Green works with larger areas to encourage creation of neighborhood parks, gardens, and revitalized communities. It has served as a model for other cities and regions of the country. Minnesota Green, for example, under the leadership of the Minnesota State Horticultural Society's Rick Bonlender, has expanded beyond the city to include the entire state. Because it is estimated that more than 50 percent of the population lives outside of metropolitan centers, it is significant that both city and rural populations participate in Minnesota Green.

The program adapts itself to each locale. In St. Paul, landscape designer Bob Harvey works with a series of shops along Como Street. He has convinced the proprietors that converting this commercial area into a flower block would be good for both business and the neighborhood. Beds beneath the street trees along the block host a delightfully old-fashioned assortment of cosmos, daisies, flowering cabbage, coleus, marigolds, and other annuals. Each bed sports a different mixture and creates a friendly, casual appearance. Residents of surrounding streets delight in walking down this block, meeting and chatting with friends. The plantings create a sense of community among the shop owners, who have become more aware of each other and of the block as a whole. These social benefits are similar to those which occur in the inner city when residential blocks join in greening programs.

Robyn Dochterman has chronicled the evolution of the Columbus Garden in St. Paul: "The garden . . . is located in a neighborhood known, not for its gardens and livability, but for crime, drug activity, and decaying housing stock. What began in 1986 as an attempt by a few concerned residents to get a burned-out apartment building torn down culminated in a project reaching across geographic, economic, cultural, and racial lines to unite neighbors, some of whom met each other for the first time while working in the garden."[7] After pressuring the city for two years, they were able to convince the owner to tear down his dilapidated building. Then they obtained permission to plant a garden, whose twenty-five plots were quickly claimed by neighborhood residents. The garden became a popular spot where neighbors met to chat with each other, comparing plants and horticultural techniques. Marie Ehrlinger, a neighborhood resident, expressed the general sentiment: "I was so proud of what it had become. It was always a treat to see what everyone was growing. I looked forward to the green and quiet and got to know people just because I had seen them in the garden so often." Much of the joy came from realizing that the community had created this haven by themselves. Tracy Bach, one of the initial organizers of the project, observed, "Now everyone walks around the garden saying this is really great. The city didn't come in and do it for us. The county didn't come in and do it for us. We did it."[8]

In 1990 the Columbus Garden received the St. Paul Garden Club award for outstanding achievement in community vegetable gardening. This is just one example of the way that gardening is increasingly being used as a tool for restoring depressed neighborhoods—the first step toward creating a sense of community and hope.

East Garfield Park is an old Chicago neighborhood. Once a handsome, well-maintained residential area with an elegant conservatory and parks, it has fallen into disrepair. The Institute of Cultural Affairs (ICA) has been working with this forty-square-block area, trying to bring it back to life. Essential to their plan is stabilizing the area, renamed Fifth City, by having residents rebuild neighborhoods and establish an economic base of locally owned businesses. They realize the need for projects that create fast, highly visible changes to serve as rallying points and maintain interest until more substantial changes can be made. ICA leaders say that they cannot start a successful community program unless people who live on a block know each other. If people are not concerned for each other, their neighborhood will not be safe.

In Fifth City, gardening is employed to inspire people to work together as neighbors. Streetside plantings of flowers, dramatically colorful additions visible both to residents and passersby, symbolize community pride and achievement. Once motivated, residents continue to upgrade the area, planting trees, repairing broken sidewalks, and, finally, obtaining loans to rehabilitate their houses. ICA calls gardening the glue that holds a block together until long-term economic and social development can take place. Because gardening helps people gain confidence in their ability to take charge of their surroundings, it is a powerful tool for coalescing a sense of community.

I do not mean to imply that the benefits of gardening are available only to people who live in urban ghettos. These examples are chosen because the smallest measure of personal gain stands out more clearly in settings of social impoverishment. The fragile beauty of flowers and the blooming of self-esteem become more vivid when contrasted against the stark background of human despair.

Gardening as *Tikkun Olam*

The progress of gardening may be seen as moving from an individualistic view, where one grows food and flowers to satisfy personal needs, to a communal view, where gardeners help and provide for each other within the confines of a physical area. The sense of community thus established leads to personal and neighborhood transformation.

The concept of sharing and healing through gardening participation flows beyond the neighborhood to include the larger community of those in need. Sharing one's produce with less fortunate people is clearly stated in the Bible (Leviticus 19:9–10), where farmers are advised not to harvest the corners of their fields nor pick up any grain that has fallen so that it be available for gleaning by the less fortunate. Now, gardeners throughout the country regularly share their produce with people in need through donations to food pantries, gardens for the homeless, or by regularly scheduled distributions to individuals.

In 1988 Seattle's well-developed P-Patch Community Gardening Program initiated "Lettuce Link" to provide fresh produce to food banks. The first year, participants grew and donated 3,098 pounds of produce. In the second year, donations and deliveries quadrupled to more than 12,000 pounds. Deliveries in 1990 exceeded 15,050 pounds; in 1991, 12,084 pounds; in 1992, 20,000 pounds; and in 1993 (a poor growing year), 17,000 pounds. In addition, they initiated the Day of Giving in 1993 for smaller garden plots. On that day, the gardeners contribute whatever they wish of their produce. It is a celebratory day, with festivities and a shared potluck meal. The Day of Giving donated eleven thousand pounds to the food banks.

The town of Huntington, New York, is proud of its outreach program, the Robert M. Kubecka Memorial Organic Garden, whose three-thousand-square-foot plot is dedicated to providing food for the needy. Volunteers donated countless hours of labor to raise two thousand pounds of produce, which they distributed to local charities. There are many other programs where gardeners share the bounty they have grown with people for whom a ripe strawberry or crisp carrot is a luxury.

Gardening directs one's view away from individuality to the reality of community; others are seen as part of the human whole. It heals, transforms, and encourages sharing. Gardens are being established in hospitals, hospices, and AIDS treatment centers. In New York City at the Terence Cardinal Cook Health Center, Fifth Avenue and 105th Street, the Tamarand Foundation brought together landscape architect David Kamp with volunteers to create the Joel Schnaper Memorial Garden, offering shaded sitting areas for AIDS patients whose medication makes their eyes sensitive to light. Low planters are available to patients in wheelchairs if they want to grow tomatoes, peppers, aromatic herbs, or flowers. The sounds of trickling water and wind chimes and the fragrances of herbs are particularly meaningful to AIDS patients, whose hearing and sense of smell are least affected by the disease.[9]

The healing and transformational qualities of gardening are central concepts of horticulture therapy. Living plants are messengers of life-enhancing qualities, and the expansion of gardening into a wide range of communities is a hopeful sign of the continuing human instinct for compassion and willingness to help others. In a society that promotes individual gain and material values, gardening presents an alternative—emphasizing a sense of community that counteracts those prevailing social and economic norms. People-plant relationships, which are innate, presage a movement toward the concept embodied in the Hebrew words *tikkun olam:* healing, repair, and transformation of the world around us.

WHY DOES IT WORK?

How does a process initiated to produce flowers and vegetables become such a strong source of personal benefit and enhanced self-esteem? What human forces are set free when a window box is planted? One clue is provided by psychiatrist Edward Stainbrook, "An environment of ugliness, dilapidation, dirtiness, over-built space, and a lack of natural surroundings, confirms the negative self-appraisal a person may have developed through other contacts with society. Self-esteem is the keystone to emotional well-being, a poor self-appraisal among other factors, determines how one treats his surroundings and how destructive he will be toward himself and others. These factors set up a vicious circle that is difficult to break."[10]

A garden immediately improves the physical appearance of any area. Although the original impetus for planting it may have been personal, it becomes a source of pleasure for strangers passing by. The gardener may be poor in material goods but is still able to give this generous anonymous gift of beauty to all who might pause to enjoy it. Doing so enhances gardeners' pride and self-esteem, which are then translated into improved feelings about the communities in which they live. Cleaned streets, painted buildings, and friendly neighbors are proof of these new attitudes.

People and plants are joined together in the garden, which is created with hands and back as well as head and heart, love, attention, and caring—all opportunities for deep personal involvement. The decision to grow a garden ignites eager expectations: Will the seed germinate? How will the peppers taste? But enthusiasm must be moderated by patience, for plants do not follow a human timetable. They must submit to larger rhythms that dictate when the seed will germinate, the flower bloom, or the fruit ripen. Through plants, gardeners are linked to the cosmic forces of life, becoming aware of being one strand in nature's web. Knowing that the pattern has been woven for millennia and will continue long after a gardener's thread runs out brings a different perspective to issues of everyday existence.

People and plants are interdependent in the gardening process. Plants receive the care and nurturing they require to thrive, and gardeners find in plants' growth a confirmation of success. Patient days of soil preparation, sowing, watering, watching, and waiting are rewarded when green leaves emerge through the dark soil. Then begins a partnership during which the two are joined in an effort to fulfill the inherent potential once hidden in the seed. Gardeners carefully watch for signals: dull, limp leaves mean water more frequently; weak stems mean add more fertilizer or perhaps provide additional light by thinning out the row. Throughout this interplay gardeners become deeply involved, learning to read the language by which plants express needs. The better that language is understood, the greener becomes a gardener's thumb.

People have an innate need for purpose, and this is addressed as gardeners assume the role of providing for their plants. The response to their care is clear, evidenced by the slow unfolding of new leaves, stems, buds, and flowers. Like markings on a ruler, this sequence of events denotes levels of successful gardening achievement.

Plants are so effective in eliciting human responses because their environment contrasts sharply with the social world in which we move. The garden is a safe place, a benevolent setting where everyone is welcome. Plants are nonjudgmental, nonthreatening, and nondiscriminating. They respond to care, not to the strengths or weaknesses of the person providing it. It does not matter whether one is black or white, has been to kindergarten or college, is poor or wealthy, healthy or ill: Plants will thrive when given careful attention. What is important is that they receive the proper sunlight, soil, water, and nutrients. Thus, in a garden, one can take the first steps toward self-confidence.

Plant growth, with its continuity and change, imparts messages concerning elemental life qualities to all who listen. Plants respond visibly to the sun. Sunflowers live up to their name by turning yellow heads each day to follow the course of its journey through the sky. Plants signal the change of season with rhythms that were biologically set in their genes by the same forces that set human biological clocks. Plant rhythms differ from those of the built environment; their growth is steady and progressive, not erratic and bizarre. With a seemingly implicit purpose, they move predictably from seed to seedling to mature plant.

Gardeners, observing the repetition of natural rhythms, become aware that change need not be disruptive or feared. Indeed, natural rhythms assure a dynamic stability. Morning glories show off early in the day and shrivel in the afternoon, only to produce more blooms at the next sunrise. We are not alarmed to see leaves turn from green to flame, sever their life connection, and fall to earth. We know that sap in spring will rise from winter roots and new leaves will burst through bark, reclothing naked branches. This happens every twelve months. We can rely on it.

How different is this from a hi-tech world in which unpredictability is a constant; where the free flow of existence is hampered, constricted, and twisted by schedule and regulation; where people must absorb the continuous assault of fads and more serious distractions; and where human life is under constant threat from human terrors and follies. Our inner selves cannot be peaceful. Deep within us lies an increasing suspicion that the living planet that nurtures us may already be irreparably damaged by the brilliant technology we have created.

Many gardening activities, such as sowing seeds, require tightly focused attention. One must be cautious with the tiny seeds of begonia or petunia, carefully tapping the seed packet over the soil in hopes of producing an even stand of healthy plants rather than clumps of spindly seedlings competing for growing space. Concentrating on this task permits no time for extraneous thoughts. Rachel Kaplan reports that this type of concentration produces a rest from the effort otherwise required to maintain attention and also provides rest from whatever worries might be uppermost in our minds.[11] Daily cares are blotted out as we carefully tap, tap, tap the envelope to release the promised life nestled inside. At that moment one is intent on the even placement of seeds in earth; it is almost a sacred ritual leading to new life.

Matthew Dumont, community psychiatrist, has tried to understand cities in terms of the mental health needs of their residents.[12] He states that city-dwellers need stimulation to break the monotony of their daily lives; a sense of community, which arises not because people are forced to live together, but rather from some spontaneous action such as creating a garden; and a sense of mastering the environment for the reassurance that they are not a helpless cog in the overwhelming machinery of living. Surely, inner-city gardening speaks to all these needs. The role of urban gardeners in promoting awareness of the importance of green nature continues to expand in urban areas. The American Community Gardening Association, at 325 Walnut Street in Philadelphia, is a haven for organizers of such community greening programs as New York City's Green Guerrillas, for example.

URBAN AND COMMUNITY FORESTRY

In addition to gardening, urban groups are taking leadership roles in planting and maintaining trees. In Los Angeles, under the driving leadership of Andy and Katie Lipkis, the volunteer TreePeople added one million trees to the cityscape before the 1984 Olympics. They continue to guide urban volunteers in caring for their urban forests.[13] Chicago's

Suzanne Hoer heads the Neighborwoods Program of the Open Lands Project, training volunteer Treekeepers, who plant and maintain their city's trees.

One can find "greens" in almost every major city in the United States, reclaiming the right for green nature to inhabit the urban landscape. This contemporary activity is perhaps a rebirth of the spirit of Arbor Day, first proclaimed in Nebraska by J. Sterling Morton in 1872, but how did the current urban and community forestry programs originate? Once an idea is accepted, we have difficulty imagining a time when it was not so. It is hard to believe that in the sixties and seventies the concepts "urban" and "horti-culture" were almost antithetical; "urban" and "forest" seemed to be at opposite ends of the spectrum. The turning point was the U.S. Department of Agriculture's Cooperative Forestry Assistance Act, passed in 1978. It mandated that the U.S. Forest Service, guardian and manager of the nation's federally owned forests, join with state foresters in establishing programs to plant and maintain urban forests. To forestry professionals schooled in the care and harvesting of wild forests, the idea was almost incomprehensible, although earlier interest in the concept was present in the Urban Forestry Working Group of the Society of American Foresters.

The new concept received further legislative encouragement through passage of the "America the Beautiful" bill in 1991, which aimed at establishing sustained, healthy community trees and forests throughout the United States for the well-being of people. Its clear intent was to involve communities and volunteers in urban forestry activities. Out of that legislation has grown the U.S. Forest Service Urban and Community Forestry Program, which brings together federal and state governments, private corporations, and professional and community groups to focus attention on establishing and maintaining trees in cities. Federal funding from the Department of Agriculture passes to state forestry agencies, which work with community officials and community groups. Each state has created broad-based community forestry councils to act as resource and advocate for expanding the programs. This structure permits a decentralized organization able to respond to local needs.

Since the original legislation, the validity of urban forests has clearly been established and is visible throughout cities as vegetation on both public and private lands. Initially conceived as the management of trees in urban areas, the concept has broadened to include the benefits of providing green for city residents, integrating the economic, environmental, political, and social values of the community. Robert Gutowski, who manages the Center for Urban Forestry at the Morris Arboretum in Philadelphia, expresses the broad view, "Urban forests are an essential part of the infrastructure of our cities . . . because our water quality, air quality, economic vitality and personal well-being are as dependent on natural resources as they are on transportation, communications and public safety systems."[14]

Trees perform a number of functions that enhance the environment: improving air quality by trapping and holding atmospheric pollutants; mitigating through shade and evaporation the urban heat island effect, reducing the energy required for cooling buildings, and reducing noise pollution by absorbing sounds that otherwise would reflect from the hard surfaces of streets and structures. Trees aid economic stability by enhancing business environments that invite people to linger and shop, and they also increase real estate values and improve personal health by relieving the psychological stresses associated with living in metropolitan areas. Urban forests reverse the steady deterioration of city life by giving residents direct contact with nature. Canopies of trees and shrubs in parks, lining urban streets, and shading yards are constant reminders of the larger forces that rule the planet.

Community aspects of urban forestry are of increasing importance. In cities across the country, volunteer groups act both as resources and advocates for expanding the programs. Trees Atlanta, Releaf Anaheim, Tree Musketeers, Green Guerrillas, Re-Tree Schenectady, Twin Cities Tree Trust, and Friends of the Urban Forest are some of the citizen coalitions that continually stoke the fires of this new green activism. Results are evident in revitalized neighborhoods, new street tree plantings, school arboretums, reforestation, and the rekindling of hope in metropolitan areas.

As with urban gardening, communities reap the benefits of urban forestry.[15] Neighbors coalesce into proactive forces, petitioning a municipality to plant trees in their neighborhoods. By working together to plan for and plant trees, neighbors gain a sense of control over their surroundings. They decide what is needed and then proceed to transform desire into reality. This may involve gaining assistance from public and private agencies, arranging for tools, digging holes, or planning and providing ongoing tree maintenance. The resulting new vegetation is tangible proof that the neighborhood cares. By joining together to accomplish their goal, neighbors gain strength and pride that is reflected in the greened streetscapes.

The communal aspects of urban tree plantings are particularly effective because each project involves both local residents and people from outside the neighborhood. City organizations such as Friends of the Urban Forest in San Francisco and People for Trees in San Diego provide expertise for communities wanting trees for their streets and yards. They help residents select species, order the plants, and obtain city permits. They even organize the planting event, assign tasks, provide planting demonstrations, and make sure each session runs smoothly.

Residents invest themselves in the operation. In San Francisco and San Diego, those who want trees must volunteer to recruit neighbors before any assistance will be given. Only after they have knocked on doors, distributed flyers, and signed up at least twenty other residents will the tree organization offer its counsel. A strong commitment by the neighborhood is necessary to assure planting success as well as continued maintenance, protection, and survival for the vulnerable new trees.[16] Planting day becomes a festival with balloons, signs, snacks, and beverages made available by the community. Trees are distributed to each planting site, then a session on planting techniques is held before residents and volunteers go to work. The whole effort is usually capped by a potluck meal at which everyone radiates pride in the splendid accomplishment they have achieved for their neighborhood. Fred Learey's sensitive report describes typical urban tree plantings in five southern California communities:

A diverse mix of residents gathers early on Saturday morning, shares coffee and muffins, and chats while they work in teams to get planting materials distributed and trees in the ground. They strengthen existing neighborhood relationships and meet neighbors not previously known. Outside volunteers meet new people while getting out of the office and improving the city environment. The children are especially quick to make friends and play. . . . For both residents and outsiders the trees are tangible objects that improve the appearance and quality of their environment. Throughout the event participants continually comment on how beautiful the trees will make the neighborhood. When the tree planting is finished, residents step back and chat with each other about what an improvement it is. They compare the area with surrounding streets that don't have trees and are excited about the future. One man said "It will be like walking in a park next year."

The trees become tangible artifacts of community cooperation. On planting day neighbors interact, thus creating a base of community cohesion. One woman chatted with a neighbor for the first time. They had lived two houses away from each other for ten years, yet never spoken. Another woman says the last time neighbors cooperated or even interacted was during the earthquake and she was very thrilled to see it happen again. Two senior women spent at least twenty minutes reminiscing about the old days in the neighborhood recalling earlier times and events in the presence of younger residents. The women had lived a block apart for at least fifty years and seldom if ever spoken. They reminisced about string telephones between houses and parents who put gates through fences so the kids could get to their friend's houses more easily. One of the most frequent comments made by the participants is that "it is nice to see the neighborhood working together." The planting also creates the possibility of future street interactions as people work to maintain the trees.[17]

Organizing and accomplishing planting day is only the first step. If newly planted urban trees are to survive, they will need continuing care for their entire lives, and participating residents are expected to continue to water and tend them. But continued tree care requires more knowledge than can be imparted in a single morning of tree planting, and in many cities volunteer groups are organized and trained to provide this quality care.

Ongoing programs for training volunteers in tree care have been established in a number of cities: Treekeepers in Chicago, Citizen Foresters in Los Angeles, the Citizen Pruner Tree Care Program in New York City, and the Master Tree Steward Program in Nebraska are examples. In Chicago, Suzanne Hoerr of the Open Lands Project leads a program that focuses on understanding urban trees, how they grow, the specific stresses they encounter (mostly from people), the kinds of trees appropriate for city sites, and their individual requirements, planting procedures, pruning requirements, and necessary insect and disease control. Graduate Treekeepers give thirty hours of service in exchange for their training. These cadres assist the municipality. Particularly where city tree budgets are inadequate, trained volunteer groups work with city foresters to accomplish maintenance that otherwise would be lacking.

Children are encouraged to participate in urban greening in their neighborhoods and on school grounds, ideal sites for the urban forest. School projects require class participation at all stages—choosing the trees, designing the plantings, and preparing for planting day and the celebration afterward. Tree planting presents opportunities for "where you are" ecology lessons. Soils, soil creation, water relationships, competition by weeds, and energy flow in natural systems all can be demonstrated as part of the exercise. Then, having invested their time and energy, the children have a strong incentive to help maintain the plants and assure their survival. Such concerns must be established early if children are to grow into adults who have a sense of kinship and respect for the natural environment. Information gained primarily from televised nature programs is not sufficient; only personal experience fully opens young minds to an appreciation and feeling of stewardship for nature. School and community greening projects provide direct contact with planting and nurturing life. In planting a tree, children establish something that will reach beyond themselves to give pleasure to others as it matures.

The full value of children's abilities to plan and carry out environmental projects has not been well appreciated. A dramatic example of what can happen when young people take charge is found in El Segundo, California, where Tree Musketeers, a children's organization, has an impact that extends far beyond the city borders. It all began in 1987, when thirteen members of Brownie Troop 91 heard a discussion of the long-term effects of disposable plastic dishes that end up in landfills. The group, hosting a jamboree for all the Brownie troops of Southern California, decided to serve their meals on paper plates that would decompose easily, but the Brownies were concerned about the trees that provided the paper to make the plates. In an effort to balance their ecological checkbook, they planted a donated sycamore—Marcie the Marvelous Tree—on a city lot. Marcie stimulated the Brownies to think about other kinds of tree activities they could create. Dubbing themselves the Tree Musketeers, they assisted individuals who wanted to plant memorial trees. They obtained the city's permission to plant on a strip between El Segundo and the Los Angeles Airport, provided instructions for proper horticultural procedures, and helped plant the initial twenty-one trees. During the next seven years, they revived the spirit of Arbor Day in El Segundo and increased the plantings (now named Memory Row) to 150 specimens.

El Segundo is bounded by an unsightly perimeter of airport, sewage disposal plant, oil refinery, office buildings, and a chemical factory. The Brownies decided to change this. Over three years they organized plantings of 650 trees that surround the city with green to soften the harsh reality. The Tree Musketeers generate their own ideas for projects. They decide what to do and then do it. They assisted the city in writing a waste management program and opened the first recycling drop-off center in El Segundo.

In 1988 the Tree Musketeers' outstanding work was recognized with an award from the Arbor Day Foundation. Since then, the group has received the Renew America Environmental Achievement Award, the President's Volunteer Action Award, and the Keep America Beautiful Award. Other children's groups have been inspired by Tree Musketeers, and they eagerly share their expertise with other youngsters through a speakers' bureau. They have discussed their projects at a White House Conference and have received requests from as far away as Alaska from youngsters wishing to initiate similar projects.

There is a growing network of youth environmental activists. Kids for a Clean Environment (KIDS FACE) has more than 110,000 members, including those from several foreign countries. The conservation activities of children offer bright hope for the future and receive strong support from the U.S. and State Forest Services, the National Tree Trust, the American Forestry Association, and many corporate sponsorships.

The work of volunteer tree groups has attracted commercial participation both locally and nationally. Global ReLEAF, a project begun by the American Forestry Association in 1988, receives support from business organizations. A study of a 1978 community tree planting project in Oakland, California, reported that business people who participate in local plantings find the reward far exceeds the cost of the trees.[18]

The National Arborist Association's donations are larger in scope. Their "National Arborists Day, a Gift to the American People" was conceived initially as a celebration of the bicentennial of the Statue of Liberty. For that first project, on April 19, 1986, professionals from twenty arborist firms arrived on Liberty Island to trim eighty-eight trees. Equipment, lunch, and imprinted shirts were supplied by the industry. This operation completed NAA's commitment of more than $50,000 in donated professional tree care to the Statue of Liberty–Ellis Island Foundation. In 1987 fifty arborists trimmed and fertilized trees at Liberty Bell Pavilion and Independence Hall in Philadelphia, honoring the bicentennial of the signing of the U.S. Constitution.

A truly memorable gift took place on October 16, 1993, at Arlington National Cemetery, where more than four hundred professionals brought their equipment to revitalize the trees shading that hallowed site. Arlington's permanent tree crew of six welcomed the help. Volunteers worked from sunup to sundown accomplishing the equivalent of $250,000 worth of maintenance. As NAA President Lauren Lanphear expressed the meaning of the gift, "by pruning, cabling and fertilizing the trees . . . we attempt to express that which we cannot put into words. By giving of what we know how to do best—to care for trees—we express our gratitude and reverence."[19]

The impact of urban and community forestry programs is both immediate and long term. The direct gain of newly planted trees and shrubs is obvious, and as the trees increase in size each year their esthetic and environmental values also increase. Their ability to shade, cool, trap pollutants, and control runoff is a continuing benefit. But those who plant and continue to care for the green sentinels also benefit. How can one measure or place value on the newfound sense of neighborliness that results from community participation in tree plantings? Once a group of people learns to control and make changes in their immediate environment, they become empowered to continue to work to improve their lot.

Participating communities lead to healthy communities. The growing trees become an ever-present reminder of their combined achievement, an incentive and reinforcement for future activities. For everyone involved, organizers, volunteers, planters, waterers, tree minders, planting trees can lead to a reconnection with the natural forces that sustain all of life. In the midst of a burgeoning technoscape, green nature acknowledges our origins, reminding us in subtle ways of our ancient experiences as we learned to survive as a species.

Young people who might want to connect with nature or pursue environmental training will no longer be forced to seek remote wilderness to learn the basics of their field. They can learn right where they live. City trees provide examples of and information on natural cycles, storm-water control, wildlife habitats, and other ecological principles. The image of untrod wilderness as sole source of information and inspiration is being replaced with the increasing acreage of urban forests.

Reintroducing green nature into cities through gardens and tree plantings can increase:

- *Social Harmony*—In community gardens, socioeconomic differences are no longer barriers. Whoever can grow the best tomato is sought out to share his or her expertise. Thus, gardening can bring together people who otherwise would never have an opportunity to meet.
- *Communication*—Organizing a window-box program, community garden, or street tree planting must be done in concert with others.

Neighbors work together to create their green magic and through the process come to know one another.

- *Friendship*—Gardens are benevolent places where shared values lead people to new appreciation for each other.
- *Self-esteem*—Through one's own efforts, plants grow, flowers bloom, and vegetables are shared. The interaction between person and plant yields feelings of success and pride in being able to make positive change that is visible to all.
- *Patience*—Plants grow according to their own time clocks. Gardeners soon learn that pace and realize that they are working in concert with rhythms that transcend human boundaries. They are put in harmony with the nonhuman forces that regulate the planet.
- *Learning*—The process of gardening requires constant attention. The unspoken dialogue between person and plant is a source of information not only about seeds, roots, and shoots, but also about our human role as coinhabitants of earth.
- *Grounding*—Through digging in the soil and cooperating with green nature, we learn to better understand our place in the world. We find our centers, loci in which we belong and can be at home.
- *Healing*—Historically, gardens have been sources of human well-being, physically, mentally, and spiritually. Gardens speak to something basic within us and help us function more easily in the contemporary world.

As Louise Bush-Brown has observed, "The window boxes and flower bays and little gardens had not only brought into these neighborhoods beauty for the eye to enjoy and a new vision for the mind to contemplate, they have also been a torch to the spirit which has kindled in the hearts of the people a striving for a better way of life."[20]

5

Horticultural Therapy

A twenty-four-year-old veteran at the V.A. Hospital in Tuscaloosa, Alabama, had stepped on a land mine in Vietnam and been totally paralyzed by the explosion. Therapists at the hospital were not convinced that his paralysis was permanent, but the patient was in despair and had stopped trying to improve. Paul Mills tells the story in the *V.F.W. Magazine:*

> One sunny day in spring, the horticultural therapist put a small glass jar half filled with peat moss beside the bed, and as the patient watched, planted five bean seeds. A few days later the seeds sprouted. Their roots were visible through the glass as they gradually extended to give life support to the tiny cotyledons working toward the earth's surface.
>
> By the fifth day the growth process was accelerating. The therapist moved the "miraculous" jar to the other side of the patient's bed where he could not see it, and instructed the nurses not to turn the patient as they had been doing. The next morning, the young veteran was lying on his other side, watching his bean seeds. Turning over had been his first voluntary movement since his accident.
>
> From that day on he made steady progress and finally was discharged from the hospital. Though still in a wheelchair, he was able to function in society.[1]

Just as the interaction of human nature with green nature can enhance feelings of peace, self-esteem, and relief from the pressures of life for people in the everyday world, it can be of enormous benefit for residents of stress-filled institutions such as hospitals and prisons. In those settings, horticultural therapy can become a gentle guide, using the magic of a germinating seed to lay a path to healing and self-confidence.

The raised bed here is made with landscape timbers set vertically in the ground. In the foreground, simple flue and sewer tiles show another way to raise the soil to a comfortable height. (Courtesy of Chicago Botanic Garden)

Major differences between the effects of urban gardening and horticultural therapy are a matter of perspective and detail. Through gardening, neighborhood residents ameliorate the trauma of social and economic handicaps, and the resulting friendliness and improved neighborhoods are large-scale consequences. Horticultural therapy, on the other hand, is concerned with people-plant interactions in a much more intimate way. Its primary purpose is to promote the well-being of individual patients, and plants become byproducts of the healing process.

A horticultural therapist works with patients at their own level of competence or need, crafting activities meant to stretch their mental and physical capacities to the fullest. Success is often measured in teaspoons: the simple task of writing plant names on labels can be a serious challenge to someone of diminished mental or physical ability. Fortunately, the repertoire of plant associated projects is wide enough to accommodate almost any limitation in agility, as are the special tools and structures now used in many institutions. At the Chicago Botanic Garden, for example, the Enabling Garden for People with Disabilities demonstrates many of the accommodations possible for individuals whose mobility is limited.

A variety of styles of beds, planters, and hose faucets are raised to a convenient height for access by wheelchair-bound individuals. Vertical planters, where a wall of bloom is created by inserting plants into wire mesh filled with a growing medium, bring gardening to wheelchair height. Adaptive tools permit digging, planting, and pruning by those with weakened muscles or missing limbs.[2]

Horticultural therapists examine every aspect of the gardening process to determine its potential for strengthening a patient's capabilities. Each procedure is broken down into its smallest component and analyzed for the benefits it might offer. Thus, transplanting seedlings can exercise fine motor control; counting the correct number of seeds, cuttings, or pots tests mental facility. A potted begonia or African violet on the windowsill becomes a vibrant symbol of life, helping transform a sterile room into a home. For long-time institutional residents, the anticipation of seeing a rosebud open or a tomato ripen is a source of joy and may provide their reason to get out of bed in the morning.[3]

Gardening tasks can be useful in evaluating the degree of handicap suffered by a patient. For example, persons unable to perceive verticals will have difficulty in relearning to walk, so patients with this problem are asked to transplant a seedling into a pot. The degree by which their planting departs from the vertical indicates the severity of their impairment.

Historically, plants have been associated with healing. Ancient societies knew the medicinal value of their native flora; indeed, contemporary scientists are trying to learn the secrets of the few remaining "primitive" cultures before they and their rain forests are erased from the planet. The therapeutic botanical knowledge of Native Americans is being seriously examined. For example, they used dogbane as a substitute for digitalis, willow bark as a source of salicin related to salicylic acid and aspirin, and dogwood as a source of fever remedies, as well as beneficial compounds from many other plants. Medieval herbalists wrote the earliest descriptions of medical and other essential uses of vegetation, and it was in order to strengthen the faculty of medicine that botanical gardens were established at Oxford University in 1621.

Until the early eighteenth century, mental patients were routinely shackled and confined indoors. Then, progressive asylum administrators brought them shuffling out of their rooms into the sunlight to participate in diversionary fresh air activities, including gardening. In the institutions that did so, patients were frequently exploited as a source of inexpensive farm labor to provide food for staff and inmates; any therapy that occurred was incidental. It took years before a few enlightened individuals perceived that farming not only helped the institution but also benefited the patient.

One of the first to comment on the connection between farming and patient health was Dr. Benjamin Rush, born in 1745 near Philadelphia. During the course of his distinguished life, Rush served as the first professor of chemistry in the College of Philadelphia, was a member of the Continental Congress, a signer of the Declaration of Independence, a member of the Pennsylvania delegation that ratified the federal Constitution, and surgeon general of the Continental Army. In 1812, while professor of medicine and clinical practice at the University of Pennsylvania, Rush noted the therapeutic effects of labor on mental patients: "It has been remarked that the maniacs of the male sex in all hospitals, who assist in cutting wood, making fires, and digging in a garden, and females who are employed in washing, ironing, and scrubbing floors, often recover, while persons, whose rank exempts them from performing such services, languish away their lives within the walls of the hospital."[4] Throughout the late nineteenth century other such statements appeared praising the benefits of outdoor labor for patients.

The Friends Asylum for the Insane opened in Philadelphia in 1817, and, from its inception, patients were involved in tending vegetable gardens and fruit trees. Their first greenhouse, a generous 72 × 24', was built in 1879. At Friends Hospital patients may still roam the magnificent landscaped grounds and participate in a strong horticultural therapy program.

In 1899 gardening was introduced as an aid to teaching mentally handicapped children. "In the garden every sense is alert. How the eye brightens at the masses of gorgeous color and the beautiful outlines. How many things hot and cool, rough and smooth, hard and soft, and of different forms are to be grasped and held by trembling hands whose sense of touch is hardly yet awakened."[5] G. M. Lawrence wrote in 1900, "Don't talk to the child about numbers; but while he is learning to distinguish one flower from another, he will unconsciously learn the number of leaves, petals, etc. And, of course, a very dull child will take pride in having *more* flowers in his own garden than a playmate has in his."[6]

The positive effect of plants on children from New York City's low-income areas was noted by Helen Campbell, city missionary and philanthropist. In 1896, describing activities at the Children's Aid Society, she cited the schoolyard of the East Side Lodging for Boys, where a greenhouse

was built above the bathhouse: "The best children in the school were allowed to take a plant home with them, and if they brought it back in a
few months, improved and well cared for, they received others as premi-
ums. Soon in the windows of the poorest, most tumble-down houses and
tenement rookeries one saw flowers growing, or met the little savages of
the district carrying a plant more carefully than they did the baby entrusted to their care."[7] Campbell mentions tenement house windows filled with
beautiful plants grown in "old tin cans with flaming labels, or small wood-
en boxes." The "flower missions" collected flowers from a variety of sources to give to the sick and poor. In 1895 more than one hundred thousand
bouquets were distributed to hospitals and homes for aged and infirm.

Through the early 1900s, health institutions used horticultural techniques as part of their treatment. By 1918 an instructor in gardening was
added to the Women's Occupational Therapy Department in Bloom-
ingdale Hospital, White Plains, New York. In Topeka, Kansas, Dr. F. C.
Menninger (whose youthful enjoyment of nature led him to a first career
as a botany teacher) founded the Menninger Foundation with his son
Karl. From the time it opened its doors in 1919, this psychiatric institution has recognized the healing qualities of green nature and integrated
botany walks and gardening projects into each patient's program. Menninger's has remained a leader in the development of horticultural therapy in the United States.

By the mid-1940s, when hospitals were established to care for returning veterans of World War II, professional occupational therapists were
joined by thousands of garden club volunteers bringing flowers and horticultural activities into the hospitals. The National Council of State Garden Clubs set horticultural therapy as one of its objectives, and 4,609
garden clubs in 36 states were conducting garden projects with patients
in hospitals or other physical and psychiatric care institutions by 1968. The
National Council's premise was that greater benefits would accrue to
handicapped individuals if instead of just being given plants they would
be involved in the process of growing them.

In Topeka, Rhea McCandliss, who had experience in landscape planting, became involved in landscaping the Veterans Administration hospital, where she started gardening classes for patients in 1946. Karl Menninger, who was in charge of the psychiatric residency program at the
hospital, wanted patients out of their rooms and into activities such as
growing plants in the greenhouse. McCandliss became, de facto, a horticultural therapist. By 1959 she had joined the Menninger Foundation as
horticultural therapist, and she developed programs for patients there for

the next thirteen years. During that time, she received many requests for information on how to use plants for therapy. McCandliss initiated a survey in 1968 to determine the extent of therapeutic plant programs in hospitals and also the potential demand for trained workers in the field. The results clearly established the need for trained horticultural therapists and the need for a means of communication among those interested in the field.

Another pioneer, Alice Burlingame, had been trained as a psychiatric social worker and occupational therapist. During the 1950s she researched and developed materials, workshop demonstrations, and articles on the use of horticulture for therapy. Collaborating with Eleanor McCurdy, the occupational therapist at Pontiac State Hospital in Michigan, Burlingame initiated one of the first programs specifically designated as "horticultural therapy." In 1960 she wrote the first text in the new field, *Therapy through Horticulture,* coauthored with Donald Watson of Michigan State University's horticulture department.[8] It took another twelve years for a full four-year curriculum to be developed. Instituted by Kansas State University in cooperation with the Menninger Foundation and now under the leadership of Richard Mattson, it provides complete academic training, including practicums for undergraduate and graduate students.

To fill the needs of the new discipline, Earl Copus, the young visionary director of Melwood Training Center in Upper Marlboro, Maryland, where horticulture is used in rehabilitation programs for mentally disadvantaged individuals, called a meeting of twenty people in the spring of 1973. Among those present were McCandliss, Menninger, and Conrad Link and Diane Hefley (Relf) of the University of Maryland. The fruit of their labor, the American Horticultural Therapy Association (established in 1973 as the National Council for Therapy and Rehabilitation through Horticulture) at 326A Christopher Avenue in Gaithersburg, Maryland, provides a professional focus for any interested person or institution, sponsoring regional workshops, annual meetings, publications, and professional registration for horticultural therapists. Stephen Davis is executive director. During its early years the organization was carefully nurtured by Copus, its first president, and Relf, who was executive secretary and then president from 1975 to 1979. As editor, she maintained the continuous publication of the group's newsletter for almost ten years.

The discipline has now moved into correctional institutions, geriatric centers, drug rehabilitation units, vocational training schools for the mentally disadvantaged, and institutions for persons with impaired sight.

Each community adapts the basic elements of horticulture to the needs of its special population.

Physical Rehabilitation Centers

How do you tell a sixteen-year-old whose last memory was of diving from a rock into a sun-drenched pool that her spinal cord is severed but there is still reason to live? Or reach the seventy-year-old man whose speech is imprisoned by a stroke-clogged brain? What magic can untwist the clawed, arthritic hands of a mother of three so that she can resume her household tasks?

These are dilemmas faced every day by the medical and support services staff at hospitals, nursing homes, and rehabilitation centers. Often the patient is too depressed to respond to the physical therapy essential for recovery. In recent years it has been found that contact with nonhuman life, such as a puppy or a cat, can be sufficient to rebuild the connective impulses that are the bridge between patient and care-givers. "Pet therapy" is being introduced into more and more of these stress situations with often remarkable results. However, many trauma patients are exhausted by or unable to follow the movements of even the gentlest creatures. With burn victims, for example, any physical touch may be agonizing. Some may have psychic wounds too deep to bear the slightest emotional demands of a purr or wagging tail. For these patients, the silent companionship of a living plant can often be the thread that pulls them back into the world.

Because a plant gives beauty unstintingly and remains steadfast, day and night, it is a beacon reminding patients of the life existing beyond their pain. Yet the plant is also vulnerable, helpless as they are. It, too, must be cared for or it will die. Many deeply traumatized patients make their first step toward recovery when they shift their focus from their own suffering to concern for the well-being of their plant.

Whether in the accident of an instant or through the tortuous process of chronic disease, there are patients in physical rehabilitation centers who have lost control or use of parts of their bodies or minds, sometimes both. Arms or legs might be absent or no longer operate to full capacity; the ability to hear, see, or speak may be impaired. In addition to physical or mental dysfunction, patients also suffer the anxiety and emotional stress that results from the impact of their loss. Eugene A. Rothert and James R. Daubert observe that "a traumatically disabled person is immediately confronted with what he cannot do. Varying degrees of dependence and of being less physically attractive contribute to demoralization and depression. This emotional suffering is not the result of the disability itself, but comes from real or imagined consequences of the disability."[9] Thus, a rehabilitation institution's programs are designed to retrain both body and mind, help patients regain use of damaged limbs or learn to compensate for their loss, and learn to function physically and psychologically at their fullest capacities. Institutional staffing includes physicians, psychologists, physical therapists, and activity (including horticultural) therapists.

At the Rusk Institute at New York University Medical Center, a generous gift from Enid Haupt in 1954 provided funds for construction of a greenhouse. Here in the "Glass Garden," interdisciplinary teams design therapeutic programs to meet the specific needs of each patient. Upon entering the hospital, patients are greeted by a cart brimming with plants and invited to select one to keep in their rooms. In making this decision, patients begin directing attention outward toward another living being and thus make the first commitment to recovery.

Dr. Joan Bardach, former director of the institute's psychological services, describes the ways that plants can help disabled individuals regain their sense of worth:

> A good portion of self esteem comes from what a person can actually do. A traumatically disabled person is immediately confronted by what he or she cannot do. Through horticulture projects the person comes to know clearly some things he or she can do because their activities produce tangible results—a plant that grows, two plants where there were originally one, etc. The disabled person has the direct experience of making a product. Another source of loss of self-esteem comes from feelings of being less physically attractive than one was premorbidly. But in growing a flower, one knows through direct experience that one can still contribute beauty to others. . . . A treatment like horticultural therapy that addresses itself to a number of levels in the person simultaneously is advantageous not just because it reflects on what happens in life, but also because the simultaneity is likely to encourage integration.[10]

Plant projects also help reduce the anxiety of patients who are withdrawn from life and institutionalized for long periods. Institutionalized people who cannot wear their own clothes or live amid their own furnishings quickly lose their sense of identity and control over their lives. But their own private space can be established by having a living plant nearby. Personal ownership of even so small an item as a potted geranium helps give the plant's owner a sense of individuality. The calming effect of plants is particularly beneficial for persons who have motor disabilities intensified by emotion. Working with plants decreases their inward preoccupation and directs their attention toward another living system—one that is completely dependent on them for its existence.

Hospital patients are bombarded by medications, injections, thermometers, and treatments that often are invasive and demeaning and always are reminders of the patients' disabilities. Horticultural projects allow them to reverse their roles: It is the patient who is in control, the plant that is the recipient of manipulation. The patient must provide for the needs of the plant—watering, pruning, and feeding. Such programs frequently culminate in the creation of a plant or flower arrangement, which the patient is then able to give as a gift. The opportunity to nurture another living entity or offer something personal to another helps soften the painful condition of constantly being acted upon. It restores a sense of personal achievement and autonomy.

Rehabilitation involves a usually onerous regimen of exercise necessary to retrain limbs and senses, but horticultural therapy can transform these sessions into pleasurable experiences. For amputees or persons who have lost the use of a dominant hand, working with living plants to relearn dominance is more entertaining than performing rote physical exercises. The many repetitive gardening tasks—watering, planting, and removing spent flowers and leaves—transmute practice with a prosthesis into an enjoyable activity. Individuals with upper-extremity weakness find that horticultural projects offer interesting ways to develop grasp and release functions and regain sensation in their fingers. Light physical activity is ideal for patients who have heart problems and who must exercise yet not overexert themselves.

Swee-Lian Yi, a twenty-nine-year-old pharmacist who suffered a severe stroke and was taken to the Rusk Institute, describes her first visit to the greenhouse. "It was when I walked through that building, perfectly quiet, filled with green and growing plants and the sweet smell of healthy soil that my anxiety began to ebb away. In its place came a tranquility I had not experienced since the day of my stroke. I started admiring cacti in bloom, and it occurred to me after a few moments that suddenly I wasn't thinking about myself and my problems. It felt like being set free."

She observed "busy people in wheelchairs, mixing soil, potting geraniums, watering and labeling plants." Their lack of conversation denoted these people as aphasics, no longer able to handle language. "I had been in their shoes so I understood the terrible frustration. What was exciting was that at least in the greenhouse, working with plants, the faces were not contorted with frustration; they were just intent on what they were doing with the plants. The greenhouse offered relief."[11] Swee-Lian Yi continued her recovery, studied the basics of gardening, and became a horticultural therapist. She has commented on the rewards of seeing clients successfully complete a task: "This great feeling is what makes me wake up every day eager to find out what is waiting for me. It could be a new rose bud forming or just a cheerful smile as the clients make their way to the greenhouse. This combination of people and plants is so beautiful and enduring it makes my life worthwhile."[12]

Success in growing plants can also provide patients with the hope that they will be able to learn to deal competently with other areas of their lives. Howard Brooks, the first horticultural therapist at the Rusk Institute, has argued that

> There will be some patients who will be difficult to reach and motivate. Working with plants may provide an impetus and initiate a response. Something as simple as the growth of roots of a cutting suspended in a glass of water or a bud preparing to open may provide the key. One of the great advantages of gardening is that it is not a static activity; there is always something happening—a new sprout, shoot or leaf is forming, a flower is opening or fading and has to be removed. Then the cycle begins all over again.[13]

Brooks notes that for many severely incapacitated patients, completely reliant on others for assistance, having a living entity depend on them for care and sustenance can awaken their will to go on and give them an interest in the future. Every aspect of the gardening process is potentially of great therapeutic value. Through staking and tying plants, a person who feels helplessly crippled because she or he cannot stand unassisted sees that other living things also need support. From an interest in supporting a plant it is but a small step to envision an interest in supporting a person. Patients discover that they, and others by implication, can find it genuinely rewarding to aid those who literally are unable stand alone.

The ability to deal with abstract concepts such as numbers and space can be assessed and strengthened through simple gardening tasks. Filling pots with soil can demonstrate spatial awareness—how quickly can one transfer soil into a pot and not have it overflow? To test numeric comprehension, a patient is given a batch of rooted cuttings, told how many to plant per unit, then asked to select the number of pots that will be needed. If this abstract calculation proves too difficult, a patient can count out the correct number of cuttings per container, place a pot beside them, and repeat the procedure. Thus, what had been a rote numbers test becomes the first stage of an actual job—planting cuttings. Other activities such as sowing seeds or transplanting seedlings require intense concentration and are useful measures of a patient's ability to focus attention. Abstract reasoning might be impaired by disease, cerebral palsy, stroke, or head wound. In those cases, tasks such as sorting cuttings according to category—unprepared, prepared, or dipped in rooting hormone—can indicate the severity of function loss.

As if trapped in a Möbius strip of gesture, brain-damaged people often tend to repeat endlessly the same unfocused movements. Through horticultural therapy, these energies can be gently redirected into useful actions. One way is in learning to cover pot drainage holes with broken shards: by starting with a single shard over a single drainage hole, then gradually training a patient to control the gesture by shifting to two, three, and four hole pots, meaninglessness can be transformed into purposeful activity.

Many perceptual problems, too, are amenable to horticultural techniques. For patients with visual field dysfunction, who cannot see on one side, materials to be used are placed on the blind side. This simple exercise helps the person to learn to turn his or her head to compensate for the loss of vision.

Horticultural therapy provides social benefits as well. Because work teams are formed on the basis of the task to be done rather than the physical impairment, patients with different disabilities participate within the same therapy group. Associating with other people to complete a horticultural project offers relief from the daily stress of striving to win personal battles. Furthermore, the horticultural skills developed can speed a patient's reentry into his or her home community, where gardening expertise is highly prized.

Bodil Drescher Anaya, while horticultural therapist at the Rusk Institute, encountered one patient who initially refused to participate in the gardening activity but would observe it from his seat outside the greenhouse. After several days he ventured inside, commenting wistfully that everyone seemed to be having fun. Anaya discovered that his hesitancy arose because he felt that he could not compete in this realm with his wife, who was president of a begonia society. Anaya therefore enrolled him into a different kind of plant project—growing bonsai. The patient, a corporate executive, soon found pleasure in controlling and manipulating his plant to achieve the desired dwarfed form. Because bonsai can live to great age, he also enjoyed the thought that someday his grandchildren might draw pleasure from what he was starting. His interest continued to develop after he left the hospital, and he later achieved recognition as a bonsai expert.

DEVELOPMENTAL DISABILITIES

When development of mental capacities becomes restricted, the ability to learn and function is impaired, and mental growth beyond that point may be limited. Progressing at a below average rate, affected individuals experience difficulties in learning, social adjustment, and economic productivity. Their degree of impairment, mild to severe, colors their ability to participate in society. Mental retardation, autism, cerebral palsy, or epilepsy can result from physiological, genetic, or pathogenic problems, often caused by use of alcohol or drugs during pregnancy. Such handicaps do not generally affect longevity, and people must therefore learn how to cope with a world geared to others who are fully functional.

The world requires people to make decisions, be able to care for immediate needs, and to know appropriate behavior and social response. Such actions may be beyond the innate ability of someone with brain damage or arrested mental development. Therapists try to help these individuals develop the maximum skills that are possible for them to achieve, and horticulture is one method employed to this end. When developing therapeutic programs, one seeks activities that match a client's age and skill level. Horticulture, a medium that transcends age, can provide appropriate projects to benefit children as well as adults. Its value lies in the inherent living nature of plants, which respond over time to the care they receive. The growth of plants offers a universal attraction that presents opportunities for interaction at a number of levels of intelligence, skill, and maturity.

Reality orientation, becoming aware of the future effects of actions taken today, is demonstrated through sowing a seed and nurturing the plant it produces. The continuous changes occurring in the growing plant are the direct consequences of having placed a seed in soil. Each physical step required—mixing soil, filling a pot, and manipulating the small object to its proper place in the pot—presents a challenge for fine motor skills. The growing seedling becomes a living lesson in learning about the sequence of events, an accomplishment achieved from a series of actions.

Matthew Frazel, horticultural therapist at the Chicago Botanic Garden, finds that subjects often cannot respond to verbal instructions, so he tries to have clients mimic his actions. He places seeds on a dark table top and picks one up on his finger. Then, he encourages clients to copy his actions until finally they understand and pick up a seed. The next step to be learned is to place the seed in a pot of soil. Each activity is broken down into small steps using hands-on demonstrations as the teaching mode. In severe situations Frazel will place his hand over the client's and move it through the actions he is trying to teach. While learning how to plant seeds, the client also gains experience in following directions.

For children, learning the basics of seeds, soil, and water is perhaps complex enough. Moving on to more advanced concepts involving plants and flowers will depend on whether the children's developmental status will permit such progress. Frazel says that one must meet clients at their own level and learn to read and understand them in order to be able to present the information in a manner they can absorb.

Working with plants can offer a stimulating change in the lives of individuals who are routinely told how to behave in every situation. Mark Smith, horticultural therapist at the Beverly Farm Foundation in Godfrey, Illinois, attempts to create a beneficial environment in which people are offered choices. He says that making decisions in life fosters self-realization about the potential for dignity, worth, and independence. For example, whenever possible he allows clients to choose which plants they will grow, thus reintroducing decision making into their lives. People must develop enough confidence to think for themselves rather than rely on others to guide their every act.

Smith tells of one man who relied totally on outside instructions to govern his behavior. One of his constant reminders had been to keep himself clean. Thus, when as part of the horticulture program he was asked to mix soil, he refused to participate. It took a year and a half of exposure to this activity, watching others carry out the task, before he was able to make the decision to dig his hands in the soil and mix it. It was a tremendous breakthrough and the start of his progress. He has since moved on to a vocational training program in horticulture.

At La Paloma Greenhouses in Corrales, New Mexico, Sid Taylor heads a horticultural sheltered workshop sponsored by the Association for Retarded Citizens of New Mexico. He believes that plants have a calming effect on clients. Although they may become violent and act out by pushing their hands through glass windows or striking staff or fellow workers, he has only once seen a client vent aggression on the plants. That happened when Taylor first came to La Paloma. He encountered a client who weighed about three hundred pounds and was in a hostile mood. They were in the greenhouse and the client picked up a pot of newly planted poinsettias and threw it to the floor. Taylor was not quite sure what would come next, but he bent over to pick up the pot, aware the client might strike him in that vulnerable position. The man's scowl changed to a look of concern as soon as the pot hit the floor, however, and he, too, quickly bent to rescue the poinsettia plants that had been uprooted.

Rehabilitation programs attempt to equip individuals with skills that can be used in sheltered workshops or in real-world employment so that they are able to maintain themselves in the greater society. Programs such as those of the Melwood Horticultural Training Center in Upper Marlboro, Maryland, are designed to bring their clients into the mainstream through placement in the field of horticulture. Their vocational training covers all the necessary aspects of holding a job—getting to the workplace, arriving on time, understanding the relationship between work and its compensation, and interpersonal relationships with other workers. The training center includes greenhouses, retail stores, and farms where developmentally disabled persons can become self-sufficient. The repetitive nature of many tasks in horticulture—watering, mixing soil, transplanting seedlings, and potting plants—are ideally suited to many developmentally disabled individuals. They do not become bored with the repetition and demonstrate patience and pride in doing their work well.

Former trainees of the Melwood Horticultural Training Center hold jobs in greenhouse production, grounds maintenance, and marketing of horticultural products. Often the plants themselves become a bridge between the worker and the general public. The natural appeal of plants often transfers to the person working with them to provide a much more vital experience than the less creative assembly-line work often found in industrial or sheltered workshop employment. Horticulture offers a path to achieving the maximum potential of many people who have disabilities, allowing them to interact as best they can with the larger community.

GERIATRIC CENTERS

Shakespeare's *As You Like It* describes the ages of man, beginning as a "child mewling and puking in the nurse's arm" and concluding "sans teeth, sans eyes, sans taste, sans everything." It is the final stage that has come under intense scrutiny as the rapidly increasing numbers of elderly in society bring their needs more sharply into focus. Concern for the aged is both societal and intensely personal. Each of us knows that if we are lucky, eventually we will join this population.

Most people over forty-five experience the frustration of being unable to recall a name or specific piece of known information, stored in memory but not immediately accessible. Such rusting of connections often signals the onset of a problem that increases with age. Loss of mental agility leads to the fear of being unable to communicate, and therefore many who suffer from it may hesitate to place themselves in situations where communication is required. That, in turn, leads to isolation from others and further loss of function. It is a domino effect that has potentially tragic consequences.

Physical deterioration, too, is a natural result of aging, but illness may be an additional cause of reduced mobility. Life for the elderly can become a prison of loneliness, isolation, and inactivity. The children whom one has nurtured have turned into adults with children of their own. No longer are they dependent on a parent's care, wisdom, love, and advice. Activities that brought interest and excitement in years past are now frequently beyond one's physical capacity. Opportunities for the very processes that endow living with zest—anticipation of future happenings, the need to make important decisions, and watching the growth and development of children—are few. Tomorrow, particularly for those in restricted environments, is featureless, nothing differentiates it from today. Lacking pointers to mark significant events to come, the future horizon is barren and limited.

Horticultural therapy programs for seniors address these problems in a myriad of ways. Gardening, even if it involves only a single plant on a windowsill, places responsibility on the gardener to care for a vulnerable life. By its dependency, the plant can become a surrogate for children now grown and moved away. Maxine Kaplan of the Ruth Taylor Geriatric Center in Valhalla, New York, tells of one resident on a home visit with her relatives. She had spent a very enjoyable few days, and, as she prepared

A volunteer in Chicago Botanic Garden's Enabling Garden for People with Disabilities demonstrates how a raised bed allows someone in a wheelchair to continue to garden. She is shown deadheading marigolds. (Courtesy of Chicago Botanic Garden)

to leave, her hosts invited her to extend her stay. "But," the woman protested, "I have all those plants in my room. They need me! I cannot be away from my babies."

Plants, predictable in their continuity of growth, clearly declare the future. One can anticipate new shoots, stems, leaves, flowers, and fruit—important rewards for the care-giver who waters and nurtures. We recognize in plants a kinship; they are a miniature representation of the creative force of which we all are a part, a connection with the other threads in the ever unfolding tapestry of life. Our need to look forward to tomorrow is balanced by the beneficial effects of remembering yesterday. Recalling times faded out of mind helps to maintain mental agility, providing an important source of intellectual stimulation.

Paradoxically, while they bring hope of the future, plants also are able to evoke the past. Their fragrance, form, or taste can trigger long-forgotten associations with people, places, and events reaching far back into childhood. The pungent smell of crushed basil, the sharpness of chives, or the delightful freshness arising from mint leaves can reawaken dormant memories of preparing family meals or of a loved one who used those herbs.

Horticultural therapy programs may take place either inside or outside of geriatric institutions. If one can handle a shovel, hoe, or rake, ground beds are appropriate gardening sites. If, however, restricted mobility prevents the bending required for working on ground beds, raised planters can be substituted. These may be constructed easily out of a wide variety of materials, from upended sewer or flue tiles to railroad ties. In raised planters, the soil surface is elevated about two feet above ground, bringing plants within comfortable reach of the gardener, who may either be standing or seated in a wheelchair. If the bed is no more than four feet across, its entire area will be accessible from the sides.

Indoor activities may include the propagation and potting of plants or making arrangements out of fresh and dried flowers (often grown by the residents). Strawflowers are particularly popular because they retain their form and color even after being cut. To exercise hand-eye coordination and fine motor skills, residents insert wires into the base of the harvested flower, creating a permanent stem. Other simple tasks, like removing dead or dying blooms and leaves, maintain healthy plants at their peak and provide the care-givers with a sense of accomplishment. Each project, whether it be producing a dish garden or creating floral arrangements and craft items, offers opportunities for making decisions and enhancing self-esteem.

In retirement facilities and nursing homes, horticulture programs can be life-enhancing experiences. Participants are motivated to leave the solitude of their rooms in order to meet and work regularly with others. No matter what their level of skill, useful tasks can be found for people to master successfully. Beginners may start by placing cuttings of an easily rooted plant, such as coleus or ivy, into a glass of water. When they determine that sufficient root development has occurred, they can plant the cutting in a pot. These simple actions require the mental exercise of judgment as well as the physical effort of handling pots and soil, planting, and watering. While creating labels for their garden plants, clients again enhance fine motor skills and mental alertness, and, by the act of writing and placing the label near the appropriate plant, they also forge a link between it and themselves. In a sense, by identifying the plant, they define their relationship to it.

Since at least the late 1940s, American society has dealt with a new form of segregation—segregation by age. One cause of this phenomenon is increasing mobility. No longer do generations stay in the same house, or even the same town. The tendency has historic precedents. The country was largely populated by adventurous, restless, or desperate people from every corner of the earth who severed close ties (or, in the case of African Americans, were forcibly severed from them) to make the perilous journey to this continent. In moving across the land, the immigrants pushed out indigenous populations wherever their interests conflicted, so that the stability of Native-American family culture has often been compromised as well.

Recent history has exacerbated the national proclivity to seek greener pastures. The uprooting that people experienced during the course of the twentieth century's numerous wars, the development of cross-continental highway and communication systems, and the proliferation of giant corporations that regularly transfer employees from city to city have all transformed the American family in profound and unexpected ways.

The family homestead, where several generations lived together, has generally been replaced by a small apartment or single-family home, just large enough for parent(s) and child(ren)—the "nuclear" family. Elders, often left behind when their children relocate, now live alone in retirement communities or institutions. Much of the rich transfer of knowledge, attitudes, and values that occurs in a multigenerational home has been lost. Many children are deprived of the rootedness earlier generations gained from their relationship with grandparents and, lacking a sense of the past, find it difficult to project a place in the future.

People can become isolated in islands of time in which each age learns only from its peers and does not have access to a longer viewpoint. Older generations find that customs have changed so quickly that they feel like immigrants in a new land—a land of youth ruled by different cultures and values. In a creative effort to ameliorate this situation, intergenerational programs are being developed to help both children and elders learn from each other and bridge the experiential gap that separates them.

One project in Atlanta, Georgia, has been particularly successful. In 1984 Jean Are, a second-grade teacher at the Westminster School, contacted the William Breman Jewish Home for the Aged to fulfill her school's objective of becoming involved in community activities. Drawing on her interest in gerontology, she and the social worker for the home developed a program in which the children and the residents participate in various cooperative projects. To initiate the program, the home's social worker comes to the school to introduce the institution and its residents to the students. Each child is asked to select a "friend," a resident with whom she or he will share an activity. Before each visit to the Breman Home, the children rehearse a song or skit to perform for their new friends. Jean Are prepares her pupils for the encounter by devoting class time to considering what life is like for older people. Answers to a questionnaire give insights into the second-graders' perceptions:

1. How old are senior citizens?
   —"over 50, 65, 50 or 60"
2. What do senior citizens do?
   —"rock in a rockinchare, rest a lot, play checkers, cards, read, talk, nit, sit and watch TV or sleep"
3. Where do people live when they get older?
   —"with there chooldren, in apartments and houses, senior citizens home, there o[w]n home or a nersing home"
4. What do older people look like?
   —"some have beards, all are blind, nice, they have ri[n]celd skin, sum wear glasses, they look nice and sweet"
5. What do older people do for fun?
   —"play with their grand chooldren, checkers, cards, watch TV, play whell of forten, ladies knit and some older people go to wirk, talk a lot, go to the market"
6. Are older people happy?
   —[most checked "yes"] "becos thay usily have copuny, there still living, have a lot of things to do, I do not no, they want to be yong again, some of them are happy and some are not"
7. Do you like to talk to older people?
   —[most checked "yes"] "it mackse them happy, they have good storys abut their lives, they are fun and nice, there still a pe[r]son and I gest like to tolk to them to mack them happy and to be nice, it is fun to linsin to there esper[ien]sis, becos thar nice"

Initially, the program consisted of one or two visits during the school year, with children and residents working jointly on craft activities. It was the responsibility of the residents to prepare clay and other inert materials used for the projects they shared with their young visitors. Throughout the rest of the year, the children were encouraged to write letters to their friends and include them in their prayers. During the program's second year, annual visits were increased to five, and Sandra Epstein, the home's horticultural therapist, became involved. She recognized that the shared activities presented a perfect opportunity for using plants.

Now, before each visit, residents select the project they wish to work on with their student partner. A particularly successful one is making dish gardens. Residents use the home's greenhouse and plan well in advance. First they choose materials to propagate, then they root cuttings that will be ready to plant by the time of the children's visit. The activity room is set up with tables in an open circle so that child and friend can sit by side to work on their project. Epstein stays in the center of the circle, available to assist everyone. Together, the partners plant the dish garden, which afterward is entrusted to child's keeping and so becomes a focus for communication between the two. Letters from the children, frequently discussing the progress of the dish garden and decorated with drawings of plants and flowers, are cherished by the residents and tacked to the walls of their rooms.

Although residents of the Breman Home suffer from a wide variety of visual, physical, and mental disabilities, their problems have not affected the program's success. Rather, their difficulties often offer important teaching opportunities. During one visit, while the group was eating together, the children observed that several of their friends were unable to control their forks well enough to prevent food from dribbling down on their clothes. Some of the youngsters laughed at the prospect of adults who could not eat without spilling their food. Back at school, the incident was discussed in depth. The children learned about disabilities and that those afflicted with the problem were terribly embarrassed by it. They were sensitized to see the situation from the view point of their friends and encouraged to empathize with them.

On Family Day, children and residents bring photographs of their families to share with each other, and the youngsters use an instant camera to take pictures of their friends. Back in the classroom, the photos become the focus for a session in which the children can tell their peers about their friend. As part of this event, the horticultural therapist explains to the children about plant families and how they are related to each other.

It sometimes happens that a friend dies during the course of the school year. When this occurs, the home advises the teacher, who, in turn, calls the parents of the child to convey the news. During class the next day, the whole group explores its feelings about the death and tries to come to terms with it. Thus, through this program, children learn to deal with matters of deepest significance—life, growth, death, grief, friendship, and compassion.

Strongly supported by parents, the program has been extremely successful. Its critical component is the teacher; children in the class change each year, residents of the home change, but the teacher remains constant. Her or his interest and initiative keep the program alive by preparing the students, handling problems, initiating letter writing, and being on hand to allay fears or misunderstandings. The children take delight in their joint projects and keeping their friend informed of the progress of their plants. Associating with young people brings a spark of joy and hope to residents. They know that they are involved with the community outside the walls, and the children learn to see them as real people instead of peculiar strangers. Sandra Epstein found that there is built-in success in intergenerational gardening, the presence of vibrant active children, their chatter, laughter, singing, breathes new life into the setting.

The experience of the program at Westminster School is equally effective when applied to community gardening, where different generations learn to know each other through the plants they grow. Such programs have obvious benefits for all involved; every plant project becomes a connection that facilitates multigenerational interaction, a focus for friendship, sharing, and communication between the partners.

Psychiatric Centers

The Chicago Botanic Garden conducts a horticultural therapy program for psychiatric patients at the city campus of Northwestern Hospital. Gardening is done in planters on the sidewalk in front of the building. One of the patients explained what it means to participate, "When I am inside the hospital I feel I *am* a big problem, but when I am outside, here at the garden, I become a person *with* a problem."

Many facets of plant growth promote the recovery of psychiatric patients. Andrew Barber, former horticultural therapist at the Menninger Clinic, Kansas has observed that "germination of seeds, vegetative growth, flowering and maturation have close parallels in the basic concepts of human development. Common gardening tasks such as watering, fertilizing and protecting plants from bad weather have human connotations. The physical structure of a greenhouse has been likened to a mother's womb and provides an atmosphere of security." He notes that activities centering around the greenhouse have helped some patients regain touch with reality.[14]

The efficacy of horticulture as therapy lies in the fact that it touches upon the broadest array of human emotions, experiences, and developmental issues of almost any therapeutic activity. People can readily compare the life-cycle of plants to their own life-cycles. "Issues of germination and birth, of nurturance and caretaking, of unexpected reversal, traumas, loss are just a few of the powerful existential dramas that can be played out in parallel fashion in both human and plant worlds. Horticultural therapy often provides the patient with an opportunity for a microcosmic reenactment in the world of plants of the kinds of struggles he or she is experiencing in everyday life."[15]

Individuals who have not been successful in the world can learn to gain confidence in the garden or greenhouse. There, working under the guidance of a trained staff, they discover that plants entrusted to their care can grow to full maturity and bloom—visible, joyous proof of their ability to succeed. As with gardeners in public housing, patients often find that plants become an extension of themselves. After investing so much time and care, they see the thriving plant as a reflection of their own being. But relationships between person and plant differ in one significant way from that between person and person. The plant cannot talk back. Barber describes a young patient who most benefited from greenhouse activity during visits from her mother. The relationship between the daughter and her "bad mother" was full of resentment and acrimony, yet in the greenhouse the patient would transform her tension and anger into expressions of deep maternal concern for her plants.

Our language reveals strong intuitive ties between people and land. We see it in the phrases "mother earth," "mother land," "father land," and "returning to the land." "This intuitive understanding about the relationship of man and earth is perhaps why the most regressed patients often find their greenhouse or gardening activity the point at which their emotional renaissance begins. . . . The parallel nature of human and plant development and the importance of earth in maintaining life is something that is understood and intuitively grasped by even the most deeply troubled of minds."[16]

The gardener-patient makes a commitment to a long-term project that requires planning for the future as well as the willingness to be consistent in caring for the plants. Deferring to the unhurried cycle of plant growth before obtaining the rewards of blossom or fruit helps patients learn about managing impulses and restraining immediate desires. Watching the steady progression of leaves unfurling and buds maturing, they can absorb a sense of the time that they may require to overcome their emotional problems and regain strength and well-being. Also, by noting a patient's responses to success (i.e., a perfect rose) and failure (seedlings that are decapitated overnight by cutworms), therapists gain insight into their character and feelings of self-esteem.

Gardening requires physical exertion, which of itself often reduces stress and anxiety. Patients who have worked away stress in this manner will be more receptive to thinking objectively about themselves. Patients who might have been frightened of one another often can work side by side in a garden or greenhouse on their individual tasks. In horticultural therapy, many projects present opportunities for "patients to enter gently into a relationship with another person in a non-verbal way, without the threat of being confronted with interpersonal closeness too soon, as may occur in a one-to-one verbal psychotherapy."[17]

The neutral plant can become an intermediary as patient and therapist communicate common concerns for its care. Martha Strauss, horticultural therapist at Sheppard-Pratt Hospital in Baltimore, says that she can learn something of the self-esteem of a patient by the size of plant they select; small plants equate with low self-esteem. She relates the comment of a suicidal patient: "I realized that I wanted to live when I took the jade plant; I wanted to see it grow." She also describes a catatonic schizophrenic in his mid-twenties who was receiving a full array of psychiatric treatment in addition to horticultural therapy. He made no contact with people and sat like a statue in the greenhouse. The therapist placed a blooming geranium in front of the motionless man and talked to him about the plant. Although he gave no overt response, the patient continued to return to the greenhouse and to the plants that were placed in front of him. Slowly, he began to interact with the plant, to touch it, finally to speak about it. In the end, he loved horticulture and was considered for horticulture vocational training.[18]

At the Brattleboro Retreat, founded in 1923 for treatment of adolescents who have psychiatric disorders, a mistake by therapist Sid Meyers turned out to be beneficial in working with his young patients. Not well-versed in horticulture, he planted carrot seeds in shallow trays and soon realized his error. Full-sized carrots could not develop in the few inches of soil he had provided. The youths were delighted to find that he had made a mistake, and it proved to be a source of bonding between the group and their instructor. This mistake was so successful that Sid Meyers now purposely plants carrots in too shallow a container in order to establish rapport with each new group.

Horticultural projects for psychiatric benefit are not limited to institutions. Across the country, special gardens provide refuge for mentally troubled individuals. At the Veterans Administration Medical Center in West Los Angeles, a fifteen-acre garden and farm—the Vets Garden—produces gourmet vegetables for trendy Los Angeles restaurants, but its more important product is peace and healing for many area veterans. The program is guided by a vivacious horticultural therapist named Ida Cousino, who took over an abandoned garden in 1985 and, with horticulturalist Bob Vatcher, created a refuge for veterans whose lives are plagued by unresolved memories—particularly of the Vietnam War.

The day of my visit in 1991 coincided with the first bombs of the Persian Gulf War. The impact of the news was felt throughout the garden, where concern was high that it would trigger the terror many veterans barely control. Warren Meyers, a thoughtful, soft-spoken veteran, explained that many of his colleagues suffer from suppressed nightmares that can be reawakened by any life-threatening crisis. He was afraid that the start of a new war would evoke such feelings and expected to hear from veterans who had left the hospital and were functioning in the outside world. He and others worked for many years to have the syndrome recognized as a separate psychological problem. Finally, in 1983, the medical profession accepted its reality and named it post-traumatic stress disorder.

As Meyers explained, the average age of Vietnam veterans when they were in the war was nineteen. During the years when they would normally have been establishing life-long values and friendships, they were suffering unspeakable horrors in combat. They were told to tough it out, suppress their fears, and go on with their lives. In previous wars, the average age of those who fought was twenty-five, and troops from the same town often traveled together as a group, saw action together, returned home together, and were able to talk with each other about what was happening to them. Vietnam was different. Young recruits were flown to their assignments alone and shipped home alone, returning, with no welcoming parades, to a nation where they were often rejected and vilified.

Most individuals learned to suppress the horrors and continue their lives until a major event trauma occurs—a divorce, the death of a family member, or birth of a child. "Then you are right back into it, back at that point you never grew beyond at age of nineteen," Myers said. For people undergoing those traumas, the Vets Garden offers a haven, a peaceful place where others with similar experiences are empathetic companions. The garden is a benevolent, life-affirming sanctuary where one can learn to function in society once more. Over and over during my visit, gardeners described the place as one where they learned to love and trust again. It was a safe community where problems could be shared. "We work as a team and help each other," one said. Although it is located near two major freeways, the secluded garden offers a quiet refuge. "Once you start working here, you just fall in love with the place and you never want to leave it. It is that beautiful and peaceful." One veteran recounted the wondrous experience of having a hummingbird drink from his hose as he watered his plants: "So safe a place."

In Vietnam, the enemy could be anyone, and no one could be trusted. A small child might innocently offer a can of soda that would be a bomb. Soldiers learned to be afraid of children, to be cruel, and to keep the children away. It is a fear that persists with many returned veterans. In order to overcome it, a VISTA program held regularly at the garden brings classes of children who have disabilities to learn and work with the veterans. Being mentors to the youngsters gives vet gardeners a way to become comfortable with and reestablish positive feelings toward children. Twice a week, VISTA also brings groups of developmentally disabled adults to work on a one-to-one basis with the veterans. Being with adults who relate to them at the level of six- to fourteen-year-olds also helps the veterans overcome some of their fear and mistrust of others.

For Cousino, the garden has been a labor of love. Indeed, one of its "products" is the love and nurturing of both people and plants. About the patients she says, "These people are always being taken care of and being told what to do—when to take their medicine, when to sleep, where to sit and when to eat. The garden gives them a chance to take care of something outside themselves and to have a feeling of success." The program helps veterans move toward the day when they can return to normal life by giving them vocational training and skills that will enable them to cope with life. The Vets Garden is proud of its strong record of graduates who have returned to school or found full-time employment, but its primary function, for hospital patients as well as veterans living on their own, is to serve as a peaceful community that helps to heal hidden scars.

CORRECTIONAL INSTITUTIONS

Gardening at correctional institutions began as a means of producing food for the prison population. The first penitentiary was built in Pennsylvania in 1821 and, like most early prisons, was located in areas with open fields on which food crops could be grown. Initially, local residents were hired to operate the farms. Then, during the 1890s when prisoners were stratified by security levels, farm labor was made the responsibility of minimum security-risk inmates. The institutions also established systems for manufacturing goods to be sold on the market, thus reducing their operating costs.

A wave of concern for individual rights during the 1960s and 1970s brought the demise of farm and manufacturing operations, as laws were passed that required that prisoners be compensated for their work and forbade the marketing of their produce or goods outside the prison system. Yet there is renewed interest in having prisoners grow plants to produce food for use within the institution, as well as for rehabilitation. Farm and gardening programs are often associated with vocational training in horticulture to provide marketable skills for inmates upon their release.

Poor self-concept is a characteristic of most prisoners' personality profile. They see themselves as failures, and people who do not value themselves have no inclination to value the rights or property of others. Researchers say that if nothing is done to affect this gloomy perspective on life, then the individual is destined for failure in society. To be effective, activities that enhance self-esteem should offer easily attainable skills in nonthreatening atmospheres, where success can be translated into positive self-regard. Gardening is such an activity.[19]

Ray Coleman, manager of detention of the Department of Corrections in Kansas City, Missouri, has commented on the positive value of horticulture: "There is nothing like watching a plant grow, seeing a flower blossom, watching a tomato ripen. It's a feeling of success. We in corrections often see this green, growing, and alive phenomenon as producing a sense of accomplishment. Plants are objects that don't make judgments. When we work with people, judgments are made all the time: 'he's good,' 'he's bad,' 'he's not so good,' 'he's not so bad,' 'he's got this weakness,' 'he's got this fault.' A flower, a plant, or a tree doesn't care what you've done or what you are. All the plant needs is the care you can give it here and now. In return for that care, it gives you a feeling of success; a feeling that you are doing something worthwhile. It also gives you a vehicle that others can see and admire. 'Gosh look at those tomatoes,' 'see those flowers,' 'what a beautiful tree.' While people wouldn't say that directly to you, they will say it about what you have done. So now you have something that other people will admire and they will reward you with their comments."[20]

The effect of enhanced self-esteem, so positive a force in inner-city gardening, is equally powerful in correctional institutions. In 1973 I helped initiate a gardening program at the DuPage School for Boys, a correctional institution for youths aged nine to fifteen. Here the boys live together in cottages and the treatment program uses the positive peer culture method. Each cottage is a close working group that functions as a unit: the youngsters eat together, go to school together, and participate together in group meetings five nights a week. Intense loyalty is created within each unit.

We instituted a gardening project at every cottage, with cottage residents responsible for their small plot. The gardens thrived, and the boys were proud of their accomplishment. Strong identification with "their" gardens became evident when one of the units was closed and several boys were moved to another building. Those who were transplanted would not accept the new cottage's garden as their own, but continued to maintain their original one despite the closure of the building. They obviously had a deep attachment to what they had planted and nurtured and did not want to lose the good feelings associated with it.

Maurice Sigler, a former chair of the U.S. Board of Parole, recounting his experiences as warden at a Nebraska penitentiary, observed that inmates might do violence to the buildings but would never destroy the plants they had grown. Robert Neese, while prisoner at Iowa State Prison, wrote, "These plants had a strangely soothing effect on our staff, when tempers did start to flare due to tension of constant confinement, a couple of hours of work in the garden made pacifists of potential battlers."[21]

In Raiford, Florida, at the Union Correctional Institution, Mark B. Jordan developed a vocational program that works closely with the Florida nursery industry. Jordan, a unique blend of horticulturist and hard-headed prison official, serves as an inspiring father figure for his students. Union inmates work in the nursery as well as operate four greenhouses in which a variety of plants are raised, including a collection of more than three thousand orchids. The inmates stage an annual flower show that attracts visitors from all over Florida. Through the program's extensive contacts with growers, Jordan's "students" are sought after for commercial employment when they are released. His program has a much lower recidivism rate than the prison's average. Warren M. Adams, a former inmate has testified to its the effectiveness:

> Garden therapy did not affect me immediately for I was a troubled soul. However within a six-month period I found myself looking forward to my work, a thing I'd never experienced. Then I started doing things which made me stop, laugh and wonder about myself. Things like not walking on the grass, singing while I worked, getting to honestly communicate and care for plants and realizing the beauty of all the life surrounding me.
>
> After progressing to a job in the Greenhouses, I matured to a tranquil entity. My moments of hate and misunderstandings became fewer. I could actually go for days without being mad at something. . . . During the last year or so of my incarceration I gave way to the calmness that was so desperately trying to enter me and started looking toward the future. . . . Prison could not break me; guards and fences could not change me; and society could not rehabilitate me. Then came garden therapy—plants, trees, shrubs, dirt, potting, mowing, pruning, planting, learning and the ever peaceful, understanding white haired supervisor (Mark B. Jordan).[22]

Horticulture is increasingly included as vocational rehabilitation in correctional institutions, often providing marketable skills for inmates after release. Prisoners are trained through formal classes and practical activities on or off the grounds. As a result, institutional landscapes are enhanced with plantings, food is provided for the kitchens, and, especially if they are permitted to sell their goods to the outside world, inmates gain a sense of pride in knowing their products have value.

Jeffery T. Philpott, vocational instructor at the Middle Tennessee Reception Center, sees horticulture as a release from the strict manipulative nature of a prison environment. Inmates, generally so powerless, regain a sense of personal control by working with plants, which respond favorably to their actions. "Gratification is realized in the time it takes to plant a seed and observe the daily change in plant growth. The constant monitoring of growth helps the inmate focus on positive thought processes instead of prison 'games' that often lead to disciplinary problems," he observes.[23]

At the San Francisco County Jail in San Bruno, counselor Cathy Snead joins with Arlene Hamilton, horticultural therapist, in crafting garden projects to augment and reinforce her counseling activities. Working with inmates sentenced to one year or less, she learned that the prison environment was not conducive to communicating positive messages about ways to improve one's life. Yet, when relocated to a garden area outside the buildings, the counseling projects become more effective. Participants, screened for violence and attempted escapes before being admitted to the program, work hard physically under the supervision of their counselor and seem more receptive to the ideas being proposed. "Outside, in the fresh air, engaged in hard, productive work, they can hear me and begin thinking about their lives. . . . The day to day chores of maintaining the plants are integrated into my counselling. I use the garden to demonstrate lessons that could not be understood through lectures and discussion alone . . . [they] learn by doing, while I explain the connection between what they are doing and how they can improve their lives and their relationships with other people. . . . The participants learn to give and receive trust, and to give and receive gratitude. . . . They begin to understand the down side of getting high on drugs, versus the up side of getting high on self respect from work and accomplishment," Snead says.[24]

Products of the inmates' labor benefit the outside world. The trees they grow grace streets in San Francisco. Food from their garden is delivered to the jail's kitchen as well as to the Open Hand Organization (for AIDS patients too ill to cook for themselves) and to soup kitchens offering meals to the homeless. Convicts find their efforts are appreciated and gratefully accepted beyond the walls, allowing them to gain self-esteem and feel that they are building positive connections to a life after prison. Through gardening, prisoners are prepared emotionally and vocationally to take their places in society with skills and work habits that will help them to find jobs after they are released.

At Rikers Island Prison near Manhattan, about a hundred inmates raise food for the institution's kitchens. Consultation with the New York Horticultural Society helped the prison farm double its productivity, so the society was invited back to develop a special horticultural training program for a limited number of adolescent inmates. NYHS's Arthur Sheppard created "Project Greenworks," a three-month curriculum that includes both classroom instruction and hands-on practice in the fields and in the greenhouse. As mandated by Operation Greenworks, participants attend classes each afternoon at the Rikers Island Academy, leading to a graduate equivalency diploma. Counseling in both job-related matters and living skills is provided to prepare the youthful offenders for release, and graduates have been successfully placed in the horticultural industry of the area. NYHS has been requested to expand the program.

The federally funded Cooperative Extension Service's Master Gardener Program sharpens gardening skills and trains students in horticultural knowledge. After completing the course, they are expected to repay their local extension offices with up to forty hours of volunteer service, such as answering telephone requests for gardening advice. Lisa Whitlesey, horticulture extension agent at Texas A&M University, brought the six-month Master Gardener Program to the Women's Federal Prison Camp at Bryan, Texas, a minimum security institution where inmates are permitted to work outside during the day. Response has been enthusiastic. Inmates are stimulated by the creative challenge of designing a garden bed plus the physical activity of propagating and growing plants. Younger inmates hope that their Master Gardener certificate will open the door to job opportunities after prison. Lisa tells of one reluctant inmate who doubted she could ever keep up with the learning requirements. After a short time, however, she "fell in love" with the program. On her own initiative, she assumed the job of labeling every plant in the greenhouse with its name, dimensions, light requirements, and description of flower type. Another inmate became so interested in propagation that she keeps a detailed record of each plant and the methods used for its propagation. As always, success instills confidence. In each program, working with plants opens new possibilities for inmates and for their futures.

Inmates who have completed the course "repay" the Cooperative Extension Service by working at Texas A&M, gaining experience that will help to find a job after their release. Master Gardener inmates work in the horticulture greenhouse, setting up laboratory materials for students, collecting research data, and monitoring the greenhouse. They also design and plant colorful beds of flowers around departmental buildings. At the prison they help as greenhouse technicians.

Qualities of Plants

Why is horticultural therapy so effective? Many other craft activities can keep patients busy and give them a sense of achievement. Why grow plants rather than knit an afghan or build a ship in a bottle? Plants and people share the rhythm of life. They both evolve and change, respond to nurture and climate, and live and die. This biological link allows a patient to make an emotional investment in a plant; however, it is a safe, nonthreatening investment. The commitment is one-way. Should the patient choose to withdraw, there will be no recriminations. In severely damaged patients, such a relationship can signify the first willingness to reach out to another living being.

Horticultural therapy is applicable to a broad range of human difficulties and provides many treatment options from which to choose. The plant world presents an almost infinite diversity of attributes—physical, biological, esthetic, and sensory. Its palette includes flowering and foliage plants, herbs, vegetables, fruits, and sprouts that can be grown from seeds, bulbs, roots, or stems. Plants are deciduous or evergreen. This diverse horticultural bill of fare offers something for everyone, the chance to select the exact combinations of factors that will best fill treatment needs.

What are some considerations taken in choosing plants for clients? How much skill is needed to be a successful grower? With a wide difference between the knowledge needed to raise an orchid and a philodendron, therapists can match a plant's requirements with the ability and condition of a client. Plants mature at different rates: marigolds and radishes are fast, orchids may take seven years from the time seed is sown until the plant blooms. For a short-term client, a rapidly growing plant is preferable because it allows him or her to experience the whole process from germination to harvest. In a geriatric home, however, the African violet's two-to-three-year development from cutting to flower might provide a more appropriate timeframe.

Plants can be selected to thrive in almost any light intensity, from bright to dim. By using artificial illumination, light conditions suitable for plant growth can be created virtually anywhere. Plants can be portable or set in the ground. A potted plant can journey home with a patient who leaves the institution, and containers are available to accommodate for ultimate size, from short to tall. Growth habits differ—not all plants grow upright. Vines such as ivy trail, although they can cling or lean on a support to become upright, providing obvious parallels for those who are dependent on crutches, braces, or other supportive devices.

Through a multiple array of controllable factors—light, shade, heat, moisture, soil, nutrients, and humidity—an individual can become more intimately involved with plants and determine their growth and performance. But none of these elements is effective without close monitoring and adjustment. Keen observation is required at both minute and gross levels. For example, insects come in all sizes; tiny red spiders are visible only if one inspects the lower surface of leaves very carefully, preferably with a hand lens. Tomato hornworms are large but usually hide during the day; one must be alert to the green pellets they excrete and the holes they chew in leaves. Plant species might be differentiated by large features such as shape or finer details such as the presence of leaf hairs.

With so wide a range of visual aspects, plant watching can easily absorb a person's full attention. Plants clearly demonstrate the normal progression of life: germination, growth, maturity, senescence, and death. Because this so closely parallels the human experience, it can perhaps help individuals accommodate to the inevitability of their own mortality. The lesson is reinforced when a dead plant is placed on a compost pile to return its nutrients to the earth. Death is part of the cycle; without it there can be no life.

The process of raising plants offers endless metaphors for human growth and development. Propagation is the ultimate in creativity—we are able to participate in forming a new living thing. Rooting equipment can be as simple as a glass of water where cuttings can be placed or as complex as a propagation bed with time-controlled misting and heat. No matter what the method used, one must learn patience waiting for the first root to appear in its own sweet time.

Plants speak of enduring values. They have existed on earth longer than people and indeed may outlast people. Crabgrass can survive a nuclear attack and keep on growing. Plants are also inherently beautiful. They speak of a sense of orderliness and progression, a kind of sanity. Offering more than visual beauty, they project a sense of peace and confer that sense of peace on those who work with them.

Cultures and languages of different lands may vary, but plants are universal. Plant growth proceeds in stages familiar to gardeners all over the world. Although the names may differ, the process can be a focus for communication with others; people often will resist instruction less when the medium is a nonthreatening plant rather than another person. The process also allows us to share ourselves with others. The gift of a carefully tended plant carries something of the spirit of the one who grew and nurtured it. This, too, is horticultural therapy, which uses every aspect of plants to help heal physical, mental, and social wounds.

6

The Restorative Environment

The increasing complexity of both technological tasks and the built environment is a source of many negative stress response patterns. In buildings, institutions, and communities, the nurturing properties of vegetation can ameliorate stress and provide maintenance for a healthy society.[1]

Through ritual, art, and myth, people have long expressed their reverence for the world of nature. The sacred groves of the Greeks were protected from desecration by humans, being sites in which the gods dwelled. Native inhabitants of the Americas recognized the reality of the natural world and their place in it; before any tree could be cut down, they would give thanks for its use and ask its spirit for pardon.

In subtle and indirect ways, we also acknowledge the power of those forces in contemporary life. Competitive society demands keeping up with the latest trends; it does not allow for the human need to rest, regain perspective, and see things as they really are rather than as we have shaped them. So, increasingly, people seek escape on paths that lead away from cities, back to places where nature rules; a day in the country is likely to be more relaxing than a day in the city. In all major metropolitan regions, those able to afford a second home usually place it in a remote area and are willing to suffer the weekly agony of bumper-to-bumper traffic to reach it. Those who do not have this escape try to spend time in public parks or at beaches. Nature is the common denominator, the universal antidote for the stress of city living.

In whatever landscape it occurs, the association of people with plants seems to be beneficial. The array of plants found in any particular area results from forces that shape the site—soil type, climate, and availability of moisture. Each plant is programmed for its niche by its ancient ecological memory, and we respond to its presence through emotion, not intellect. The setting—woodland, prairie, or desert—speaks directly to us; we simply feel it.

WILDERNESS EXPERIENCES

Woodland settings are archetypical representations of the natural world, different from the built environment in which daily routines occur. Camping, contending with the lack of facilities and comforts, demands digging deep within ourselves to find other resources than those we draw upon in urban life.

Outward Bound, brought to the United States in 1961, uses wilderness as the context for programs of personal development, giving participants a series of tasks that require them to develop new skills and learn to rely on themselves and others in their groups. Through accomplishing these personal challenges, they gain an enhanced awareness and appreciation of their abilities.

I remember separate visits by a niece and nephew as each came out of an Outward Bound trip. The teenagers bubbled over in sharing their incredible experience, what it meant to them, and what they had learned about nature and themselves. Both considered their "solo" as the high point of the adventure. Alone in the woods for three days, totally dependent upon inner resources, they were forced to look deep into themselves, and they were elated to discover new personal strengths and a sense of rootedness in the natural world.

Living in wilderness is basic to many restorative programs geared to specific populations, whether composed of corporate managers, educators, juvenile delinquents, or psychiatric patients. In each case the individual does not compete with others, but tries to raise personal standards of achievement. In the natural environment they are challenged to discover their untapped potential.

Wilderness camping programs were originally developed for mentally ill youngsters who had negative self-images and whose needs were unmet by traditional treatment in an office setting. The structured outdoor experiences were all aimed at aiding them to better cope with their feelings and behaviors. Participants learned to fulfill individual responsibilities while becoming functioning members of a group.

Andrew L. Turner has reported on two such programs: the first provided a positive springboard for nine boys who survived five days in the wilderness.[2] The experience helped them work out their problems as well as identify and maintain better interpersonal relationships with their peers and with the two counselors who shared the adventure with them. The second program involved a group of patients in a Maryland State hospital. After being hospitalized for more than two years, they had lost motivation to progress or work toward their discharge. The group was placed in a wilderness camp for two weeks and encouraged to prepare meals, wash clothes, spend money, write letters, and relearn other social behaviors. "Within three months of the experience 41 of the original 90 patients had been granted discharges and one year later only 2 of the 41 had been readmitted."[3]

Of course, one need not be emotionally disturbed to benefit from being in nature. For most people, the idea of a vacation implies a change of scene and pace, a time of respite. We long to find a different landscape, to break from the daily routine and roam free in a world where human influences do not predominate. Natural systems create the context when we leave the incubating spaces of urban structures and their controlled environments. Vacationing in nature makes people more keenly aware of their surroundings; weather and water speak more directly. "Thoughts that lie too deep for tears" may be provoked by contemplation of simple elements, be they grains of beach sand, water-burnished pebbles, seeds, tiny mosses, or giant redwood. We can return from these holidays physically and mentally renewed, ready to resume the challenges of daily life.

In hypnotherapy, the trance state is achieved through an induction process. Patients are asked to imagine themselves in a calm, peaceful scene. Most often, they conjure up memories of mountains, forests, fields, lake shores, and oceans. Picturing themselves surrounded by nature creates the relaxed, tranquil state of mind that is most receptive to the treatment.

Foresters and psychologists are trying to unravel the riddle of the restorative qualities of green nature. During a ten-year study, environmental psychologists Rachel Kaplan and Stephen Kaplan, with the help of Janet Fry Talbot, a graduate research assistant, analyzed the effects of a wilderness trip in Michigan for high school students and adults. The trip featured many of the elements of Outward Bound, such as making one's way in a new unexplored wilderness setting and gaining such survival skills as orienteering, camping, cooking, and woodsmanship. In a solo experience, each camper (equipped with a piece of clear plastic for shelter, a hunting knife, salt, and a survival cup for cooking) was sent off to a remote location for forty-eight hours. Each was asked to maintain a detailed diary of the activities carried out and the emotions they experienced. After returning home the campers continued their journals for two weeks and completed questionaires. The trips presented a superb opportunity to learn about the kinds of feelings that arise during a retreat from civilization. Over the ten-year period, the Kaplans and Janet Talbot were able to tease out the human factors at work when a person takes off for the woods.[4]

Away from the distractions of the daily world, many campers were able to explore new facets of their personalities. In addition to learning to survive without a car or grocery store, they were "learning new ways of thinking and learning their way in the world as a whole, learning of the compelling relationship that can exist between the world and each individual."[5] The journals reveal the emotional progression that most participants underwent during their adventures:

Day 3 —Fears arise about the weather and coming activities. The smells, sights, and sounds around them are noticed more keenly. They begin to feel more comfortable in their surroundings.

Day 4 —Accomplishment of tasks is acknowledged along with complaints about personal difficulties, ranging from blisters, bruises, and insect bites to the "torture" of rough hiking. But there are joys, too: "terrific" sleeping, swimming, and eating, feeling refreshed and invigorated, and "having a blast."

Day 5 —A sense that this is more than an enjoyable experience in the woods is implied in comments about a new sense of competence, the ability to handle whatever difficulties might arise. They are "free and happy and relaxed" and feel a sense of peace and tranquility.

Day 7 —Participants feel a wondrous new sense of themselves and the surrounding environment, which leads to thoughts about spiritual meanings and eternal processes. They feel "different" in some way—calmer, at peace with themselves, "more beautiful on the inside and unstifled." Privacy is cherished as a time when they can consider their own thoughts rather than being concerned with other people's activities.

Days 9–11—Solo is an encapsulated rerun of experiences that occurred from the beginning of the trip. Alone, there arise feelings of uneasiness. As night falls, sounds that were familiar at camp seem more ominous ("I thought i herda bare but it was a fly"). Anxieties give way to a sense of enjoyment, which develops into exhilaration and awe and, finally, a deeper understanding of their surroundings and place in that natural scheme of things.

Through these journal entries, the Kaplans were able to gain insights into the restorative qualities of natural settings. One important finding was that self-perceptions and perceptions about relationships to the natural world change. Living in wilderness draws attention to small details of the landscape that previously would not have been noticed or appreciated. The surroundings become comfortable, and people are surprised at how easily this sense of belonging has happened. As Kaplan and Talbot report, "There is a growing sense of wonder, and a complex awareness of spiritual meanings, as individuals feel at one with nature, aware of the transience of individual concerns when seen against the background of enduring natural rhythms . . . they feel more sure of who they are and what they want to do."[6]

A heightened sense of spirituality seems to be inherent in the nature experience; it is as if a gate opens to a deeper self-understanding and sense of connectedness with larger forces in the universe. This is reported time and again, whether by campers, Outward Bound participants, or visitors to the Morton Arboretum. Clearly, experience in nature resonates deeply within; it somehow helps to intuit hidden personal pathways that can be explored and appreciated.

But what happens when the happy campers return to the commonplace activities of daily life? Does the memory of that uplifting experience remain fresh in their minds although they are no longer in the wilderness? The Kaplans report that the insights the participants acquire are largely retained.[7] Their woods experience gives them a different perspective on "normal" activities; decisions made during the camping experience are seen as vital, necessary for continued functioning and actual survival. Day-to-day concerns at home seem to be more trivial. The contrast between the natural and the urban environments emphasizes the artificiality of the places in which they usually live. By comparison, the constructed landscape now seems ugly and boring. Deep within they feel more closely tied to nature and the new selves they had discovered there. When compared with the pressures of home, the woods are remembered as peaceful and relaxed. City-bound campers often make plans to return.

As a result of the sensitivity developed during their wilderness experience, campers become more aware of the presence of nature in the

city—for example, bird songs, gardens and parks, or wind in the trees—
and seek walks or weekend trips that bring them into contact with these
reminders. New goals include wanting to remain physically active and in
shape and to retain their self-confidence. The sense of cooperation and
mutual trust developed during the woods trip is remembered fondly. Back
in their normal environment, the campers seem to have a sharper ability
to discriminate between the significant and unimportant.

> The memory of their time in the wilderness seems to serve as an emo-
> tional benchmark. . . . They know that tranquility is possible; that there
> is room for more than the present, for more than immediate urgen-
> cies, in their thoughts. They see new possibilities for disregarding some
> of the demands of their everyday environment; for substituting their
> own purposes for the goals that society urges on them; and for choos-
> ing their own activities rather than those more commonly pursued. In
> many ways, the participants' view of themselves, as well as their per-
> spective on the world, has increased in scope.[8]

Substitutes for Wilderness

Wilderness studies clearly demonstrate that intimate contact with a
natural green environment twenty-four hours a day can affect people
positively. But must they be surrounded by it to feel the difference? The
Kaplans wondered about "micro-restorative environments," the smallest
representation of wilderness that could offer restorative qualities. Might
there still be a favorable effect when we can only apprehend the natural
environment through a window? What happens when people must spend
time in windowless rooms? How do they compensate for the lack of a
view? These issues have been examined in studies of diverse settings, including prisons, hospitals, and even space stations.

What has emerged is that even a brief encounter with nature can be
restorative. My experience confirms this; I have found that even a momentary glimpse of trees outside my office window helps reduce stress.
Countless times during the day I find myself glancing up almost reflex-
ively at their pattern of trunks, leaves, and branches. I am not thinking
about the trees, but just seeing them refreshes my mind.

Roger Ulrich of the College of Architecture at Texas A&M University
has been able to establish that the sight of trees out of a hospital window
has beneficial effects on the recuperation of surgical patients.[9] He re-
viewed the records of patients of similar age and condition who had

undergone the same operation. Their major difference was that one group occupied rooms whose windows offered the prospect of trees, whereas the others looked out on a brick wall. Ulrich's analysis compared the length of hospital stay required for recovery, the amount and strength of pain killers required, and the patient's attitudes about their surgery and the nurses who tended them. The differences were dramatic. Recuperating patients who could see trees required less—and milder—pain medication. Their feelings after surgery were more positive. They were more pleasant to nurses and other care-givers and were released from the hospital after fewer days than patients with the view of the wall. Just seeing green nature was beneficial for patients and, by shortening their hospital stay, it resulted in a monetary savings as well.

The view from a window also affects the well-being of prison populations. In institutions serving the dual purposes of incarceration and rehabilitation, the environment is necessarily restrictive. Noise, crowding, personal criticism, social discrimination, heat, cold, and intrusion into privacy are all beyond the inmates' control. They must contend with the threat of harm from other inmates, separation from home and family, long hours of confinement, and little daily activity. Their choices for coping with this life are either to adapt or become ill. The greater the tension, the more likely they are to report on sick call, complaining of hyperventilation, itching, headache, backache, excessive muscular tension, nausea, or chest pain. The rehabilitative function of the institution is impeded by the stressful aspects of incarceration.

Outer-facing cells are more likely to have views of vegetation and landscape than are interior cells that face other facades of the building. Cells on upper floors will more often allow a view over the walls to see what lies beyond. Two major studies have analyzed the kinds of views seen from prison windows and compared them with the frequency of sick call for the inmates.[10] Researchers have assessed what could be seen—vegetation (fields, farmland, or mountains), buildings, or combinations of both. Inmates whose windows allowed them to see beyond the prison, particularly those whose view included natural elements, took fewer sick calls than inmates of cells that faced other buildings.

It seems apparent that mere visual contact with nature beyond the prison walls can help reduce stress. This is not surprising. The only readily available means of escape from cell confinement is through the mind. The inmates' world expands with what is seen outside their windows, allowing them to project beyond their immediate surroundings and submerge the reality of incarceration. If the view reflects only the prison, there is no opportunity for visual escape. Looking out a window to see more of the prison only verifies the grim truth of their situation. But when the view projects beyond the walls, particularly to scenes of nature, the imagination can savor a sense memory of the natural world in which we arose as human beings. Marcia West says, "The natural view is an important lifeline to people who are restricted in their daily experiences. Visual contact with green spaces creates the opportunity for mental niches—isolated, calm and restorative backwaters."[11]

The restorative quality of green views is increasingly being understood in such stressful environments as hospitals, nursing homes, remote military sites, space ships, and space stations. Studies also show that seeing nature is important for people who work in offices without windows. When decorating these spaces they choose almost four times as many photographs or posters of outdoor scenes as do workers in offices with windows. More than 75 percent of the visual representations in windowless offices include no buildings or man-made artifacts at all.[12]

At the Edward Hines Jr. Veterans Administration Hospital outside of Chicago, the Laboratory Services Department occupies a large area that includes both windowed offices and interior laboratory spaces. Concentrated here are all of the hospital's laboratory services, including pathology, chemistry, microbiology, and the blood bank. Plants are everywhere. They sit on windowsills and drape themselves over filing cabinets. The cold sterility of the scientific laboratory is softened by green foliage growing with abandon among microscopes, analytical equipment, hoods, and bottles of chemicals. Atop a tall cabinet storing chemical supplies is the habitat for two pots of trailing pothos, which cascade gracefully down its sides. One does not expect to see a poinsettia sharing space with a microtome or a hanging basket of ivy adorning the ceiling above laboratory benches. But here, the austere world of science is successfully invaded by the almost rambunctious fertility of growing plants. I had to smile when I first saw them doing their irrepressible thing in this technological space.

The laboratory operates twenty-four hours a day, and its lights provide these green mavericks with sufficient artificial illumination to keep them healthy. Larger plants brighten windowless conference and waiting rooms. The haphazard garden is a joint project of Gregorio Chejfec, M.D., chief of laboratory services, and Tom O'Donoghue, manager of laboratory services. Initially, they brought plants in as "environmental monitors" to determine whether the indoor air might be contaminated with formalin from the laboratories. None was found, but the greenery thrived, and the scientists and technicians enjoyed seeing it. Slowly, the plants migrated out to their present locations in the laboratories and offices. One person, Nancy Barred, who is the timekeeper and honorary "plant pathologist" provides the loving care that helps this remarkable garden to flourish.

Chejfec says that the plants have made a difference in the ambience of the area, which is reflected in the attitudes of the people who work there. They feel special because their environment is enhanced. The presence of plants in the stark, windowless conference rooms has improved the quality of human interactions that take place there. The home-grown greenery differs from that found in office buildings and other settings where professional interiorscape companies maintain the vegetation. In those situations the plants are usually well trimmed, almost regimented, and shaped to be picture-perfect. At Hines, they are free to trail informally or find their own form. Their casualness of growth adds a quality of friendliness and relaxation to the laboratory setting.

Another high-tech interior is found on craft that fly missions to outer space, where some remain as manned space stations and others return to earth. NASA has sponsored research to document what kind of experience these cramped environments offer to occupants. In the early days of space flight, information was available from pioneering American Skylab astronauts and Russian Salyut cosmonauts.[13] Their quarters were confining, filled with vital technological apparatus. Almost all sound was mechanical; fans, motors, pumps, computers, and uptake vents switched on and off, and voice contacts with ground control offered a distant human resonance. For the astronauts and cosmonauts, cut off from all that was familiar, it was important to try to maintain some emotional link or a sense of attachment.

They dreamed predominately of landscapes, mountains, and clouds. A cassette recording of sounds from nature was particularly welcome; the space travelers never tired of it. Projecting slides of outdoor scenes, accompanied by bird songs and the sound of rushing water, helped reconnect them with earth. Such audio-visual representations were able to ease the fatigue and emotional strain inherent in life in a space capsule. It seems that one does not have to experience actual nature; tapes and slides can successfully evoke restorative mental images and associations. Landscapes created in the imagination can be an effective antidote for relieving stress.

Measuring the Restoration of Green Nature

In comparing a glance out of the window with total immersion in wilderness, we find that even the less intense experience is beneficial. For years, Roger Ulrich has been interested in the short-term effects of nature scenes. His interest lies in what people like to see and how the view affects them. He has not been satisfied to rely only on psychological tests in which people check off the degree of preference for a scene or indicated how they felt at a given moment. The body reacts to what the eye beholds, and Ulrich wants to measure those changes as they occur, to record continuously how the body responds to stressful situations and recovers to a restored level.

Measures such as blood pressure, tension in muscles, and excretion of stress hormones such as adrenalin are indications of physical response. These increase when we are excited or stimulated—part of the old fight-or-flee mechanism that helped to sustain us through the tough times of evolution. The extra adrenaline that prepared primitive humans to fight off danger or escape quickly continues to stimulate our internal system whenever we hear a sudden noise or see a threatening situation.

Ulrich knows that our complex bodies are governed by more than one nervous system. Elevated blood pressure and heart rate are produced by the sympathetic nervous system, which prepares a body for action. It uses energy and therefore is fatiguing. But humans also have another nervous system, the parasympathetic, which works in the opposite manner to slow heart rate, lower blood pressure, and increase activity of the digestive tract. This restores and maintains body energy. Both systems belong to the autonomic nervous system, which largely governs the body's internal environment, keeping it in balance during periods of stress and recovery. They are part of the exquisite organization that allows the body to function without conscious supervision.

Because all aspects of human beings were calibrated during evolution in natural environments, the body as well as the mind should react positively to the environment it has known since its beginnings. But urban environments are relatively new. When our ancient stasis is confronted by new situations to which it is not adapted, our bodies respond with stress—not for automatic functions alone but often for emotional and cognitive states as well. "Modern humans have a biologically prepared readiness to quickly and readily acquire restorative responses with respect to many unthreatening natural settings, but have no such preparedness for most urban or built contents or configurations."[14]

Ulrich wanted to test the hypothesis that nature scenes should have more restorative influences than urban scenes. He first subjected all participants to emotional stress by showing them a video depicting the horrors of work accidents. Then they were divided into six groups, each of which viewed a different ten-minute tape to test its effectiveness for restoration. All videos were of everyday outdoor settings. Two featured nature scenes of trees and other vegetation, water, and trees, and four were urban, with two-way heavy traffic, light traffic, an outdoor shopping mall with heavy pedestrian traffic, and a mall with light pedestrian traffic.

Throughout the testing period, monitors continuously recorded blood pressure, heart rate, skin conductance measuring the activity of sweat glands, and tension of the frontalis muscle in the forehead (which is activated by the central nervous system). In all cases, positive restoration as measured by physiological functions occurred more rapidly and was more complete for persons viewing the nature scenes rather than urban scenes. The nature scenes produced evidence of a recovery action in the parasympathetic system early in the period. This did not occur with urban scenes. Psychological tests taken at the end of the session corroborated the physiological tests: People who saw nature scenes reported being more relaxed than did those who viewed urban scenes.

Restorative Qualities

To understand the restorative qualities of green nature for humans, we must once again return to their connections. A green world was our teacher at a time when the species' survival was a continuous challenge. The sight of living vegetation stimulates the neural pathways established then, so we are biologically prepared to feel a sense of connection with green environments. But what has happened to our surroundings? In the timeline of evolution, early humans had a long apprenticeship in natural environments. The time to learn to dominate that environment and reshape it has been much briefer. The first cities are only a few thousand years old, whereas our innate responses to nature go back to the dawn of human history.

We have not spent enough time in our new surroundings to replace our preferences for primitive habitats and allow the ancient neural pathways to be reset. Although we find proper habitat in buildings with water and sanitary systems, and the local supermarket is a ready source of food, such things have not existed long enough to influence a change in the innate mechanisms shaped by our beginnings. We are still biologically tuned to prefer those settings in which we learned how to survive.

That green environments satisfy intuitively can be verified among many of the cultures on earth. When people of diverse backgrounds are given a choice between scenes of nature and scenes of buildings, nature wins out. If asked to choose between urban scenes with or without vegetation, settings that include plants are selected. This is our genetic heritage at work, preferring landscapes that are evolutionarily most familiar. Psychiatrist Edward Stainbrook points out the wide range of impacts on innate human systems in accommodating to the newer ways of living:

> Having evolved through aeons of living with nature, organisms including man are genetically programmed to biological rhythms paced by sun, moon, and seasons. Hence we are often out of phase with modern situations—with artificial lighting, central heating and air-conditioning, with work organizations and other social institutions structuring wakeful activity around the clock, with distressingly demanding sleep-disturbing attempts at mastery, with rapid travel through time zones. Fatigue and inefficiency and perhaps more subtle impairments of adaptation and biological responsiveness may be the price we pay for disharmony between the body's innate rhythms and the artificial surroundings and demands that press upon us.[15]

How might daily living provoke stress and its resultant mental fatigue? Few are free to daydream, just letting thoughts drift free. Instead, there are rigid schedules to meet, projects to complete, and work to accomplish, often in situations in which we must try to meet standards set by others. Throughout the day we try to stay focused on what we have to do. If all is compatible, the day might go very well. When the environment is not compatible, however, one must pay increasing attention to the task at hand and try to screen out distractions. An office partner who wants to chat when we are in the midst of preparing a detailed report, a child clamoring for attention, the noise of traffic on a nearby street, a radio playing too loudly, or thoughts anticipating an evening's activity after work can all interfere. If we are unable to stop the distraction at its source, then we attempt to block it from our mind. We concentrate on what we should be doing, trying to screen out all extraneous thoughts and noises. Hard work, even when mental, can lead to fatigue.

Similarly, if we are to solve a mathematical equation or try to understand a difficult passage of text, the presence of distractions would force us to use energy to screen them out. Solving a math problem or discerning the meaning of a passage of text can be an invigorating experience—if we are allowed to do it. But if the environment is hostile, we must constantly struggle to focus on what we intend to do. Then pleasurable tasks become onerous, and the mental facility that screens out conflicting stimuli becomes fatigued. The inability to eliminate distractions can lead to reduced competence, irritability, loss of judgment, and antisocial behavior—the price we pay for an environment at odds with our chosen goals.

Some sources of mental fatigue, although subtle, also complicate daily existence. The simple act of walking from one point to another can be mentally stressful because the urban environment presents endless stimuli: street signs designed to capture attention, the aroma of hot dogs with sauerkraut wafting from a curbside stand, signal lights, store window displays, and surging traffic. If we succumb, sampling the ambience, we might never reach our destination. To keep ourselves on track, our minds must be selective, directing our attention only to those stimuli important for accomplishing the task at hand. If we can successfully put on sensory blinders, chances are we will arrive on time.

We are all familiar with this need to focus consciously on a specific action. However, a different kind of attention occurs when we are in deep contact with something we find inherently interesting. We can be "lost" while listening to music, reading a good book, watching television, or solving a challenging crossword puzzle. It is not necessary to deliberately concentrate, because the activity itself is so entrancing that we become absorbed in it. Time passes quickly and intruding thoughts are blocked out. Surprisingly, when our minds return to the everyday world, we are not exhausted. On the contrary, this kind of involuntary attention is refreshing. Probably one of the reasons that golf appeals to so many is that it requires undivided focus on each shot. There is no chance to think about other problems; the entire being is concentrated on addressing, swinging at, and hitting the ball so that it will satisfactorily fulfill the trajectory we envision. And it all takes place in the fresh air of an outdoor green setting.

Nature itself can entrap us involuntarily, occupy our minds, shut out daily cares, and allow us to become refreshed. There is something mysterious about the natural world. We can stretch out in a field of daisies, look at the clouds in the sky, or watch an ant crawl to its hole in the ground among the grasses. We can walk through fields, explore forest trails, and be fascinated by the surroundings. Yet these activities may not be so encompassing as to demand all our attention; our minds can remain open to other things. Slowly, the sense of green nature overrides outside distractions. While thus relaxed, we can allow our thoughts free rein, as did the visitor to Morton Arboretum who, after walking for hours in those verdant woods, was finally able to accept the death of a loved one.

Green nature represents a world of which we are a part, yet it is distinct from the one we inhabit daily, where everything is under human control. Green nature is not duplicitous, it does not scheme or display human vices. The natural world is rich with overtones expressed in its inherent order and organization. In it we sense an underlying structure in which diverse parts fit smoothly together. The green world's depth can be explored both physically and mentally. Start with a tiny pollen grain, and it will lead you to the concept of forest. Nature organizes itself into living layers: a canopy overhead, a middle story of smaller trees and trunk-climbing vines, shrubs, and, finally, close to the earth, annuals, perennials, and ephemerals that peak in spring and autumn.

Green nature is self-correcting and self-directed as long as outside forces do not obliterate its underlying, life-sustaining network. When a natural disturbance occurs—a tree falls or fire burns through—the system immediately begins to repair itself. The explosion of Mount St. Helens devastated miles of surrounding countryside, yet now new plants are everywhere, re-covering the blighted land. If the impact is too great, however, such as occurs with wholesale cutting and burning in the rain forest, the ecosystem's inherited intelligence, built over millennia, is crippled. Recovery is then a long, desolate, and unpredictable road.

The diversity of green nature is evidence of an independent living system that has been developing since its inception many millions of years ago. Acorns have been leading to oak trees for a much longer time than humans have been cutting them down. In this system we recognize a counterpoint to our technical prowess, reassurance that human constructs are not the only way. Green nature acts like a conscience, telling us that we must realize that our civilization is not necessarily life's highest achievement, that without chlorophyll and sunshine we could not exist. The vine covered ruins of Machu Pichu and the barren hillsides of Haiti are eloquent testimony to the long contest between human and natural forces.

Our bodies and minds have been, as Ulrich says, "biologically prepared" to respond to landscapes that helped set our physiological and psychological patterns. Seeing green nature and participating in activities such as gardening obviously enhance our well-being. Knowing this, would it not make excellent sense to try to create micro-restorative environments in stressful spaces? More sensitive siting of buildings to give a view of nature, planting trees and gardens in urban areas, and providing plants in offices, hospitals, and other tension-producing spaces will help make us feel at ease in a technological world. These reminders of ancient origins are links to the world from which we emerged and our bodies still know. The presence of vegetation in urban places could help to reduce the strain of living in a culture that we have created but that remains largely alien to our innermost selves.

7

Toward a Green Tomorrow

This book has traced the history of our relationship with plants, from the time when they formed the nurturing context for our emergence as a successful species to their ambiguous status today in much of the inhabited world. Even though humans like to think of themselves as being in control of both nature and society, it may be that they have now arrived at a point where success will overwhelm them. Can we relearn to care for the world of green nature? What will the future decide?

MEDICAL FUTURES

The scientific scrutiny of green nature will surely continue to play an important role in the future. From the beginning, plants have provided balms to ease pain and illness, whether taken orally in medicines, rubbed on in salves, laid on in poultices, or imbibed as teas or infusions. Medical research continues to probe their individual chemistries for sources of cures as yet unknown.

One of the imperatives for preserving tropical rain forests is the near certainty that such cures are waiting to be discovered in the uncharted jungle. However unexplored medicinals are found in less exotic settings. Taxol, a derivative of the bark of yew (taxus) endemic to the Pacific Northwest, has been found beneficial in fighting ovarian cancer. This exciting news carried with it the immediate danger that all surviving taxus stands of the region would be sacrificed to obtain the drug. Fortunately, scientists have been able to create a synthetic form of Taxol thus saving the species from destruction.

When Hurricane Andrew flattened Florida's famed Fairchild Tropical Gardens, site of a valuable collection of exotic plants, immediate action was taken to ship samples of the felled vegetation to laboratories to be analyzed for useful compounds. Perhaps good will be distilled from disaster in the form of new medicines derived from those plants. In any event, the green world will continue to be examined as a source for botanical healers.

One promising new area deals with programming plant genes to produce antibodies previously available only from mammalian blood serum. It seems possible that tobacco, whose link with cancer has gained it a notorious social and medical reputation, can become a factory for bioengineered pharmaceuticals and other chemicals. Tobacco is a fast-growing plant that produces a large amount of foliage. It is highly susceptible to tobacco mosaic, a virus that spreads virulently but does not survive outside the tobacco plant. Taking advantage of these characteristics, the expanding field of genetic engineering is putting tobacco into service to humanity. This comes at a propitious time for tobacco farmers, for the connection of smoking with cancer and emphysema has reduced cigarette consumption in the United States and seriously limited areas where one may pollute one's lungs and the ambient air with equanimity.

Antibodies, the proteins antagonistic to specific disease organisms, were initially produced in the blood serum of horses, rabbits, or pigs. Traditionally, diseases such as diphtheria and tetanus have been controlled with injections of these sera, which can cause serious reactions when given to anyone sensitive to animal proteins. A new era of treatment began in 1975, when biotechnologists succeeded in developing monoclonal antibodies that are more precise in their action, binding to specific sites on disease cell molecules. Because the antibody attaches itself to very specific sites in the cell, it may become one of medicine's most powerful weapons against the scourge of cancer and be used to identify deviant cells and perhaps carry radioactive isotopes to destroy them.

These designer antibodies are produced commercially in vats of bacterial solutions, but techniques are being developed to explore tobacco's ability to replace bacterial hosts. Andrew C. Hiatt of the Research Institute of the Scripps Clinic in La Jolla, California, has successfully transferred the desired antigen gene into the genetic components of tobacco, where it then directs the plant to create the correct monoclonal antibody.[1] At harvest, the antibody can be extracted from the tobacco for medical use. Most important, the plant's ability to make the new material is passed on to succeeding generations through normal seed production. Monoclonal antibodies thus created are free of any mammalian taint that might adversely affect sensitive patients. Hiatt estimates that antibody production in plants would cost one hundred to one thousand times less than current bacterial methods. Other advantages come in the manner of storing the producing matrix: Bacterial cells must be maintained at the low temperatures of liquid nitrogen, whereas the tobacco source could be stored simply as seeds.

In another demonstration of biogenetic skill, researchers at Biosource Genetics Corporation in Vacaville, California, have developed the ability to insert genetically altered proteins into the genes of tobacco mosaic disease. Healthy stands of tobacco are inoculated with the altered mosaic gene, which spreads rapidly throughout the planting. Within a month the plants can be harvested and the genetically engineered proteins extracted. Initial experiments have included tests for production of an AIDS drug, a component of human blood, and an enzyme used in food processing. Because the engineered protein is carried only in the tobacco mosaic virus, which deactivates when the plant dies, the process is inherently safe against unwanted spread of the altered virus. Biosource Genetics hopes soon to have an extraction plant in operation to start production of the bioengineered proteins.

Mich B. Hein, also of the Research Institute of the Scripps Clinic, hopes to produce a substitute for the usual method of immunization accomplished through injections. Among his projects is the transfer of specific antibodies to alfalfa, which could be dried and when eaten produce the desired immunity. It could be shipped to countries in Asia and South America, allowing the widespread delivery of immunity to even remote areas and replacing the need for sterile syringes and the refrigeration of serum.[2]

Using plants as factories to create vaccines, immunoglobulins, and other medical proteins, substances that might have come from animals or perhaps endangered plants, opens a bright and unlimited horizon. In addition to providing drugs traditionally obtained from them, plants will be assuming a new role, producing chemicals not even indigenous to their biology. The full range of applications is enormous; pest and herbicide resistance, veterinary and human pharmaceuticals, novel separation systems including waste-water treatment and degradation of toxic waste, and antibody based therapeutics are all being explored. This is only a tantalizing glimpse of the ways in which plants, usually considered as sources of food, fiber, and structural materials, may be employed to sustain humankind.

POLITICAL TWISTS

Concerns about the well-being of plant communities can become strong political issues. Many of the green movements in the United States and in Europe evolved in protest to environmental degradation and its effects on all life. But this positive desire to protect native or indigenous plants can have unexpected ominous overtones, as was evidenced in Germany. During the early 1900s, a burgeoning concern for native plants was expressed by a drive to eliminate non-native vegetation from German gardens. This twentieth-century evolution of concern for native plants into a racist attitude about land and landscape is charted by two contemporary German landscape architects, Gert Groening and Joachim Wolsche-Bulmahn.[3] For example, rhododendrons were declared aliens, to be removed from all plantings. The same attitude was shown toward other imports, such as Chinese forsythia.

During the twenties, this horticultural xenophobia was easily incorporated into the racial ethic of Aryanism espoused by the National Socialists. During the early stages of its development, National Socialism twisted popular interest in growing native plants into the credo that only German plants were suitable for the German race. They soon extended the concept even farther, saying that the landscape responds to the racial purity of its inhabitants. In their takeover of Polish lands to the East, they "proved" their point with photographs showing that those lands had been degraded because the Polish spirit did not express itself in a pure landscape. "The 'highly developed requirements' of German people concerning landscape, which corresponded to the close bond to nature, had to be contrasted with the lack of a feeling for nature displayed by other people and races, which as a result were declared inferior. This helped justify the reformation of the conquered areas as well as the conquest itself and the expulsion of native population: genocide developed into a necessity under the cloak of environmental protection."[4] Plans were drawn up to "Germanize" the acquired territory to ensure that Germans who resettled there would dwell in a landscape that reflected their racial superiority. Groening and Wolsche-Buhlman cite "Rules of the Design of the Landscape" developed by the planning staff under Heinrich Himmler:

For Teutonic German man, dealing with nature is a deep need of life. In his old native land and in the areas which he has settled and formed with the vigor of his people [*Volkskraft*] over the generations, a harmonious picture of farmland and garden, of settlement, of fields and landscape has become a criterion of his being. . . . If the new living spaces are to become a home to the settlers, then the well planned and close-to-nature design of the landscape is a prerequisite. . . . It is not sufficient to settle our people in those areas and to eliminate foreign people [*Volkstum*]. Instead the area must be given a structure which corresponds to our type of being [*Wesensart*], so that the Teutonic German person will feel himself to be at home, so that he settles there and is ready to love and defend his new home.[5]

These perceptions of landscape reflecting the "spirit" of the inhabitants were part of the propaganda distortions that accompanied all expressions of the National Socialist program.

Groening and Wolsche-Bulmahn have documented the social manipulation of landscape, ecology, conservation, and gardening of the Nazi era, but their purpose is to warn of the ever-present danger inherent in the politicalization of seemingly acceptable ideas.

Environmentalism and protection of natural habitats, currently strong themes in world politics, are susceptible to being co-opted by groups whose intentions may not reflect the benevolent concerns of the majority of their followers. By the same token, those for whom protection of the environment is seen as an obstacle to greater profit may assume the mantle of concern for nature, as the wolf assumed the sheepskin, to confuse the public into supporting policies that will result in continuous degradation of the ecological systems upon which all life depends. It is important that we take nothing at face value but try to learn who is speaking, what they stand to gain or lose, and what they really are saying.

People-Plant Relationships: An Emerging Concern

As a people-plant horticulturist, I have represented a minority viewpoint. Horticulturists generally believe that the discipline should be concerned only with plants, growing or selling them to achieve economic or esthetic goals, leaving the human component to other professions. I had not anticipated how difficult it might be for academic professionals to accept a different way of seeing horticulture. They failed to realize that their profession exists because of people, including themselves and all other horticulturists, who are interested in plants. Most of academic horticulture views horticultural therapy, which acknowledges the importance of people-plant interactions, as an uncomfortable companion, outside the realm of scientific horticulture. Therefore, to pursue my interest in the human aspects of horticulture, I had to look to other disciplines—psychology, sociology, geography, and medicine—which focus on people and their behavior. On several occasions I was the only horticulturist at a national meeting or conference, yet my viewpoint was always welcomed. I found colleagues in those fields who had no difficulty in accepting the significance of the fact that people respond to plants, and, with their encouragement, I was able to continue to seek the human meanings of ghetto gardens.

Since the 1960s, my search has expanded beyond flower beds and window boxes into the larger landscape of forest, meadow, and woods. Concurrently, awareness of its human aspects began to dawn on a small group within the field of horticulture. Initially fueled by horticultural therapy, the growing interest was also spurred by a few young horticulturists, particularly those with a city orientation who were touched by the human benefits they witnessed in gardening programs. For years we were horticulturists without a home for our people-plant views. By the mid-eighties, however, a broad, multidisciplinary base was emerging for people-plant relationships. Attention was called to the new emphasis through a series of symposia; "Improving the Quality of Urban life with Plants" was conducted by the New York Botanical Garden in 1985; and Mark Francis and Randy Hester brought together diverse viewpoints to speak to "The Meaning of Gardens" in 1987.[6]

It became evident that we needed to meet formally with the psychologists and other professionals interested in people-plant relationships. Diane Relf organized the first multidisciplinary symposium, "The Role of Horticulture in Human Well-Being and Social Development," which was held in Arlington, Virginia, in 1990.[7] At that event, representatives from psychology, geography, sociology, horticulture, landscape architecture, and architecture shared their expertise about people-plant interactions in human culture, communities, psychological studies, and horticultural therapy. At last, horticulturists could have discussions with other professionals whose primary interest was the way people respond to the environment. The mixing of these diverse views acted as a catalyst, producing great enthusiasm. Horticulturists found that their concerns for people, of little interest within their own departments, were welcomed and highly respected by others. At structured sessions and through informal conversations, a bond was forged, creating a vibrant constituency that had a vital new focus.

From that symposium has emerged the field of human issues in horticulture. The People-Plant Council, chaired by Diane Relf, was established in 1990 and is based at 407 Saunders Hall at Virginia Tech University in Blacksburg. It serves as a network of continuing information and direction. A second symposium, "People/Plant Relationships: Setting Research Priorities," was held in 1992, and the third, "The Healing Dimensions of People-Plant Relationships," was held in 1994 at Davis, California.

An increasing interest by academic and professional horticultural organizations is evidenced in the creation of committees on human issues in horticulture by the American Society for Horticultural Science and the American Association of Botanical Gardens and Arboreta. In 1994 the International Society for Horticultural Science, meeting in Kyoto, Japan, included a symposium titled "Horticulture in Human Life, Culture and the Environment" with presenters from the United States, Europe, and Asia. At that conference, an international committee was formed that will study human issues in horticulture under the aegis of the International Society for Horticulture. Even the new horticultural research agenda of the U.S. Department of Agriculture includes people-plant interactions.

At last, horticulture is acknowledging the power of its human aspect, a reality long familiar to its gardening practitioners. And, because governmental bodies are more impressed by hard data than by anecdotal evidence, a continued expansion of research can be expected that will delineate and quantify the beneficial effects of people-plant interaction.

Ideally, plants will become more integrated into culture. The environmental psychologist Steven Kaplan looks forward to the "social acceptance and appreciation of people's spending time, even during the 9–5 day, in natural settings as a competence and productivity enhancing activity rather than as an example of moral degradation and wasted time."[8] Plant-centered activities will become accepted as a standard part of the rehabilitation treatment in prisons and drug rehabilitation centers, and will be a deterrent for children heading for gangs and violence. Reestablishing the people-plant connection will be seen as a priority for a healthy humanity.

Conclusion

Every plant and animal demonstrates a different way of life. . . . What we share with them, however, is at least as profound as our differences. We are all participants in the planet's experiment in living. If we can understand what that means then human self-interest and the preservation of other creatures [forms of life] becomes one cause and one connected experience.[1]

The next veil to life which may be lifted is humanity's avoidance of [its] feelings about nature.[2]

The essential point I hope to establish in this book is the critical relationship between humans and green nature. As a species, we have arrived at a place where our childhood dependency on nature has largely been replaced by a more sophisticated vision: We are in charge, free to shape the world for our own progress and well-being. We see ourselves as separate, within a purely human context. Green nature is no longer teacher-partner, but servant and often opponent. This view fails to grasp the reality that humans are just one of a multitude of diverse life forms inhabiting the planet, all participants in its "experiment in living." As Ian McHarg comments, "We can only be enlarged by accepting the reality of history and seeing ourselves in a non-human past, our survival contingent on non-human processes."[3]

We have difficulty abdicating our self-proclaimed superiority to the rest of nature. People in the West seem caught in the belief that nature is primarily a resource to be used for our benefit. After all, are we not at the top of the heap? The question we should be asking concerns what kind of heap we are constructing. Is all well in the technosphere of our creation? We are squandering the accumulated capital created during the lifetime of this planet, fouling the very nest that gave us life.

Our magnificent cities are nourishing for only a favored few. For the rest, our culture is one of ever-increasing stress. In the United States, for example violent crime has increased by 560 percent since 1960. Disciplinary problems facing school teachers in 1940 included talking out of turn, chewing gum, cutting into line, and violating the dress code; in 1990 the top problems facing teachers were drug and alcohol abuse, rape, robbery, assault, and pregnancy. Teen suicide has increased by more than 200 percent.[4]

I believe that part of the reason for these increasing symptoms of dysfunction is due to the fact that we have severed connections with our evolutionary roots. They represent a mismatch between innate physiological and neurological needs and the results of technical prowess. As a species that lived most of its life surrounded by elements of nature, within recent history we have transformed our habitat into high-density cities of brick, stone, glass, concrete, and asphalt. Our ancient selves are out of sync with what has recently been created. The drastic changes in how we live have not had time to be absorbed into the systems that slowly evolved within us.

Edward O. Wilson uses the term *biophilia* to identify the force that ties us to nature, a love for nature, and the life it represents.[5] Yet, many deny the wisdom that has helped humanity to survive. David Orr observes, "The human mind is a product of the Pleistocene age, shaped by wildness that has all but disappeared. If we complete the destruction of nature, we will have succeeded in cutting ourselves off from the source of sanity itself."[6] Human attitudes toward nature are redefined by changing cultural and social patterns. In the older concept, humans were caught between the God-centered view of heaven and hell, walking a narrow path between the two. Everything on earth was either an opportunity or a temptation leading to one of these destinations. During the latter half of the seventeenth century, the God-centered view was replaced with an anthropomorphic view that placed humans in control of nature. Earth was perceived as "a perfect, maintenance-free machine designed by God as home for these bipedal creatures made in his own image: the human race. . . . Everything in nature was made for human use and accommodation . . . the new view treated Earth as an ergonomic vehicle. We call the ergonomic vehicle spaceship Earth."[7]

Our culture has made clear its attitude toward nature as a resource. Soil, water, air, minerals, and vegetation are available for domination, and we have cast our rapacious net to include them all. We must climb out of our anthropocentric skin to view ourselves in a nonhuman context as part of the total expression of life on this planet. People and plants are inextricably bound together. It is time to acknowledge our dependence on the system that traps the energy by which we live and whose echoes are internal reminders of our evolutionary childhood. We must understand ourselves as dependent on that from which we arose, not as its conquerors. We who are now destroying the very biological diversity that cradled us must open our eyes and recognize ourselves as a species that carries within its neurons memories of survival landscapes.

We have only begun to see dissatisfaction with the effects of human domination, a rising suspicion that somehow the vast storehouse of nature, our birthright, might become depleted. Future generations may not have available the horn of plenty we have known. These concerns may be the harbingers of a new definition of human-nature relationships, a view that is life-centered, biocentric. "We are starting to sense that human beings are no longer at the center of Earth's purpose. Our species is, rather, one integral aspect of the greater interdependent network of nature."[8] The biocentric view can lead to a greater appreciation of our role as participants in the "experiment in living," helping us to see and accept ourselves as part of the total expression of life.

Ancient patterns laid down during our primitive beginnings are evidenced when we respond to seeing a tree, watching seeds germinate or finding restoration in green nature. They provide insight into our kinship with the biodiversity of the planet, a need to respect it to prevent our own succumbing to the status of an endangered species. We have been responsible for the vanishing of hundreds of species of animals and plants through overhunting, pollution, and destruction of habitat. Acres of rain forest—the planet's lungs—are being cut down daily, exterminating species before we even have a chance to catalog their existence. Yet, we do not know our own fate if the extinctions continue.

Homo sapiens learned to survive by listening to and learning from nature. Acknowledging its reverberations within us leads us beyond the symbols of our apparent success as a twenty-first-century civilization to the basic truth that we are still creatures dependent on earth; whatever we inflict on the planet, we inflict on ourselves. If we are to continue to survive as a species we need to acknowledge this connectedness to all life.

Refusal to acknowledge this reality leaves an emptiness within. It is much like the phantom pain from a cut-off limb. As the body "remembers" its missing part, so do we miss our dimly remembered connections with nature, and as physical deformities may be caused by lack of particular nutrients, so can psychic deformities be caused by lack of psychic nutrients found in those ancient connections.

Because we are preconditioned for an affinity to vegetation, it is not surprising that throughout history we have loved plants. We should remember that the preconditioning took place over millions of years, but our ability to step outside ourselves to look at this affinity is most recent. I believe the simplest path to this awareness is through exploring people-plant relationships, which acknowledge our connections with nature. Personal experiences with green nature point to a hidden dimension in life. It is not recognized cognitively or intellectually, but it occurs at a deeper level of humanness, dimly perceived and difficult to articulate clearly. Our ancient brain, which helped to select a safe habitat, still functions. We must peel away the layers of intellect that obscure what is remembered in our genes: Green nature and human nature are both expressions of the pervasive life force that permeates the planet.

This is the viewpoint of many indigenous peoples and Eastern cultures who see a unified creation in which life is the diverse embodiment of elementary energy. The Chinese call it *chi;* for Native Americans it is "the breath." They consider themselves as a link in the great chain of existence, kin to clouds, trees, animals, land, streams, and flowers. People and plants are but different aspects of that life force. Hopefully, Western societies will also come to understand that they are part of the total tapestry, much of which is woven with living, green threads.

When we garden, grow plants, or find tranquility in park or forest, the ancient processes are at work within us. It is time to acknowledge them and explore their significance for our continued existence. They point the way to a new appreciation of ourselves as strands in the fabric of life woven throughout the world.

There must be humility on our part, acknowledgment that any impairment of that fabric ultimately will impair us as well. If we can act in accordance with this understanding, we may be able to heal some of the wounds of our increasingly aggressive and fragmented society.

All that has happened to the planet as a result of human residence is real. We cannot turn the clock back to an age when our effect on nature was less, nor would we want to become hunter-gatherers again, accepting whatever gifts nature might offer. Once the pristine is damaged, it cannot be restored. We live here, now, in this place, at this time. And as we look to the future, we must enact decisions which will further affect the environment.

Michael Pollan suggests that we become gardeners of the planet, working with nature to achieve our goals and knowing that we must revere the soil and water or they will not provide sustenance.[9] Gardening is really a partnership in which we try to understand a plant's needs and make certain that they are met, aware that whatever we do impacts nature.

Can we extend that metaphor to a planetary scale? Can we regain our reverence for the Earth, care for it so that it will continue to nourish us? Can we learn to live lightly on it?

We stand at a fork in the road of the Holocene epoch, the last 3.5 seconds of that thirty-minute film documenting the history of Earth. We can continue to rape the land to extract its mineral wealth, pollute the oceans, cut down the forests for short-term food production, and destroy vegetation and fresh-water lakes with acid rain and pollutants. Or, by acknowledging our ancient and intimate connections with green nature, we can become aware of our participation in the flow of life energy. We are writing the next chapter in the history of our civilization; will it be a new beginning or the end?

The Greek legend of Antaeus speaks poignantly to us: Antaeus, the giant son of Terra (Earth), was a mighty wrestler, whose strength was invincible so long as he remained in contact with his mother. Hercules encountered him, and, finding that it was of no avail to throw him—for he always rose with renewed strength from every fall—lifted him up from the earth and strangled him in the air.

Deep within each of us lives Antaeus, our mythic bond with mother Earth who nurtured and sustained us throughout the millennia of our evolution. Yet, relentlessly, day by day, the Hercules of technology is separating us from our lifesource, covering Earth's green skin with concrete and asphalt.

We are counseled: do not sever connections with the natural world in which we arose as a species. The ties are ancient, and without them, like Antaeus, we may perish. Consider the trees, the soil, the water, the air. Heed the faint stirrings within, responses to green nature that remind us of our long-forgotten emergence into consciousness as homo sapiens. They were locked within our genes by the same forces that first set human biological clocks and the life rhythms of this planet.

Native Americans believe that every living thing tells its own story. At a subjective level we can hear the continual murmur of green speaking to our psyche from fields and forest, weeds and wildflowers, gardens and window boxes.

Chlorophyll is our continuing connection with life that comes from the sun. Plants are telling us the story of the universe of which we are a part.

But will we listen?

Notes

Chapter 1: Green Nature

1. William Wordsworth, "The Rainbow," in *The Oxford Book of English Verse,* ed. Arthur Quiller-Couch (New York: Oxford University Press, 1940), 624.

2. Frederick Law Olmsted, *Notes on the Plan of Franklin Park and Related Matters* (Boston: Department of Parks, 1886), 107, as quoted by Charles E. Beveridge in "Frederick Law Olmsted's Theory of Landscape Design," *Nineteenth Century* 3 (Summer 1977): 41.

3. Diane Ackerman, *Natural History of the Senses* (New York: Random House, 1990).

4. Jay Appleton, *The Experience of Landscape* (New York: John Wiley, 1986).

5. Barbara Ward and René DuBos, *Only One Earth* (New York: W. W. Norton, 1972), 12.

6. Barry Lopez, "Ecology and the Human Imagination," in *Writing Natural History: Dialogues with Authors,* ed. Edward Leuders (Salt Lake City: University of Utah Press, 1989), 22.

7. Aldo Leopold, *Sand Country Almanac* (New York: Oxford University Press, 1949); Ian McHarg, *Design with Nature* (Garden City: Doubleday, 1971), 43.

Chapter 2: Green Nature and Human Evolution

1. Gordon Orians and Judith Heerwagen, "Evolved Responses to Landscapes," in *The Adapted Mind: Evolutionary Psychology and Generation of Culture,* ed. Jerome H. Barkow, Leda Cosmides, and John Tooby (New York: Oxford University Press, 1992), 557.

2. Richard H. Wagner, *Environment and Man* (New York: W. W. Norton, 1971), 5.

3. Roger Ulrich, "Natural versus Urban Scenes: Some Psychophysiological Effects," *Environment and Behavior* 13 (September 1981): 523–66; Stephen Kaplan, Rachel Kaplan, and John S. Wendt, "Rated Preference and Complexity for Natural and Urban Visual Material," *Perception and Psychophysics* 12, no. 14 (1972): 354–56.

4. Rachel Kaplan and Stephen Kaplan, *The Experience of Nature: A Psychological Perspective* (New York: Cambridge University Press), 1989.

5. Roger Ulrich et al., "Stress Recovery during Exposure to Natural and Urban Environments," *Journal of Environmental Psychology* 11 (1991): 201–30.

6. Roger Ulrich, "Aesthetic and Affective Responses to Natural Environments," in *Behavior and the Natural Environment,* ed. Irwin Altman and Joachim E. Wohlwill (New York: Plenum, 1983), 86–125.

7. Stephen Kaplan, "Environmental Preference in a Knowledge-seeking, Knowledge-using Organism," in *The Adapted Mind: Evolutionary Psychology and Generation of Culture,* ed. Jerome H. Barkow, Leda Cosmides, and John Tooby (New York: Oxford University Press, 1992), 590.

8. Appleton, *The Experience of Landscape.*

9. Jay Appleton, *The Symbolism of Habitat* (Seattle: University of Washington Press, 1990).

10. Stephen Kaplan and Rachel Kaplan, *Cognition and Environment* (New York: Praeger, 1982), 75.

11. Orians and Heerwagen, "Evolved Responses to Landscapes."

12. Ibid.

13. Ibid., 559.

14. Herbert W. Schroeder and Thomas L. Green, "Public Preferences for Tree Density in Municipal Parks," *Journal of Arboriculture* 11 (September 1985): 272–77; Rachel Kaplan, "Dominant and Variable Values in Environmental Preference," in *Environmental Preference and Landscape Preference,* ed. Ann S. Devlin and Sally L. Taylor (New London: Connecticut College, 1984).

15. John D. Balling and John H. Falk, "Development for Visual Preferences and Natural Environment," *Environment and Behavior* 14 (1982): 5–28.

16. Balling and Falk, "Development for Visual Preferences," 5.

17. Aaron Latham, "To a Stranger, Africa Feels Like Home," *New York Times Magazine,* November 10, 1991, 33.

18. Gordon Orians, "Habitat Selection: General Theory and Application to Human Social Behavior," in *The Evolution of Human Social Behavior,* ed. J. S. Lockard (Chicago: Elsevier, 1980); Gordon Orians, "An Ecological and Evolutionary Approach to Landscape Aesthetics," in *Landscape Meaning and Values,* ed. E. C. Penning-Roswell and David Lowenthal (London: Allen and Unwin, 1986).

19. Annie Dillard, *A Pilgrim at Tinker Creek* (New York: Harpers, 1974), 33.

20. Rose S. Solecki, "Shanadar IV: A Neanderthal Burial Site in Northern Iraq," *Science* 28 (1975): 880–81.

21. Wordsworth, "The Rainbow," 624.

Chapter 3: Green Nature Observed

1. Dee Hansford, *Gardens of the Walt Disney World Resort* (Orlando: Walt Disney World Co., 1988), 8.

2. Charles Lewis, "Nature City," *Morton Arboretum Quarterly* 11 (1975): 11, 17–22.

3. Beveridge, "Frederick Law Olmsted's Theory of Landscape Design," 40.

4. Victoria Ranney, *The Papers of Frederick Law Olmsted*, vol. 5: *The California Frontier* (Baltimore: Johns Hopkins University Press, 1990), 428.

5. Victoria Ranney, *Olmsted in Chicago* (Chicago: R. R. Donnelley, 1972), 7.

6. "Indenture Made 14 December 1922, Establishing a Foundation to Be Known as the Morton Arboretum," typescript, Morton Arboretum Archives, Lisle, Illinois.

7. Tony Hiss, *The Experience of Place* (New York: Knopf, 1990), 1.

8. Herbert W. Schroeder, "Preference and Meanings of Arboretum Landscapes: Combining Quantitative and Qualitative Data," *Journal of Environmental Psychology* 11 (1991): 231–48.

9. "A Bloedel Reserve Overview, June 29–30, 1990, Philosophy and Purpose," unpublished pamphlet, Bloedel Reserve, 1990.

10. Prentice Bloedel, "The Bloedel Reserve: Its Purpose and Its Future," *University of Washington Arboretum Bulletin* 43 (Spring 1980): 4.

11. Bloedel, "The Bloedel Reserve," 2.

12. Lawrence Kreisman, *The Bloedel Reserve: Garden in the Forest* (Bainbridge Island, Wash.: The Bloedel Reserve, 1988), 45.

13. Prentice Bloedel, "An Interpretation of the Objectives of the Bloedel Reserve Preliminary to the Preparation of a Master Plan," unpublished notes, July 14, 1983, 1.

14. Herbert W. Schroeder, "The Felt Sense of Natural Environments," *Proceedings*, Twenty-first Annual Conference of the Environmental Design Research Association, Champaign-Urbana, Illinois, 1990.

15. Eugene T. Gedlin, *Focusing*, 2d ed. (New York: Bantam Books, 1981), 32.

16. Schroeder, "The Felt Sense of Natural Environments," 192.

17. Herbert W. Schroeder, "The Experiential Benefits of Urban Forests," in *Making Our Cities Safe for Trees: Proceedings of the Fourth Urban Forestry Conference* (Washington, D.C.: American Forestry Association, 1990), 38.

18. Neil Evernden, "The Ambiguous Landscape," *Geographical Review* 71 (April 1981): 155.

19. Paul Shepard, *Man in the Landscape* (New York: Alfred A. Knopf, 1967), 236.

CHAPTER 4: PARTICIPATION WITH GREEN NATURE

1. Kaplan and Kaplan, *The Experience of Nature*, 167–71.

2. Ibid., 168.

3. Ibid.

4. Robert M. Hollister and Christine Cousineau, *The Greening of Boston: An Action Agenda*, ed. Mark Primak. Report from the Boston Foundation/ Carol R. Goldberg Seminar (Boston: The Boston Foundation, 1987), 64; Lyndon B. Johnson, *Beauty for America: Proceedings of the White House Conference on Natural Beauty* (Washington, D.C.: Government Printing Office, 1965), 2.

5. Louise Bush-Brown, *Garden Blocks for Urban America* (New York: Charles Scribner's Sons, 1969), 11.

6. Bush-Brown, *Garden Blocks for Urban America*, 28, 32.

7. Robyn Dochterman, "The Columbus Garden," *Minnesota Horticulturist* 119 (January 1991): 31–33.

8. Dochterman, "The Columbus Garden," 32, 33.

9. Kathleen McCormick, "Realm of the Senses," *Landscape Architecture* 85 (January 1995): 61–63.

10. Edward Stainbrook, "Man's Psychic Needs for Nature," *National Parks and Conservation Magazine* (September 1973): 23.

11. Rachel Kaplan, "Some Psychological Benefits of Gardening," *Environment and Behavior* 5 (1973): 145–52.

12. Matthew Dumont, *The Absurd Healer* (New York: Viking Press, 1968).

13. Andy Lipkis and Katie Lipkis, *The Simple Act of Planting a Tree* (Los Angeles: Jeremy P. Tarcher, 1990).

14. Robert Gutowski, "The Basics of Urban and Community Forestry," *Public Garden* 9 (January 1994): 10.

15. Richard G. Ames, "Urban Tree Planting Programs: A Sociological Perspective," *HortScience* 15, no. 2 (1980): 135–37.

16. Robert Sommer et al., "The Social Benefits of Resident Involvement in Tree Planting," *Journal of Arboriculture* 18 (May 1994): 98–101.

17. Fred Learey, "Themes of Community Participation in Tree Planting," *Proceedings*, Healing Dimensions of People-Plant Relationships Research Symposium, Department of Environmental Design, University of California, Davis, 1994, 383, 388.

18. Richard Ames and A. W. Magill, "Urban Trees: A Link to Social Wellbeing," *Proceedings*, Society of American Foresters Annual Meeting, Boston, 1980.

19. Lauren Lanphear, in Peter Gerstenberger, "National Arborist Day," *Tree Care Industry* 4, no. 11 (1993): 40.

20. Bush-Brown, *Garden Blocks for Urban America*, 11.

CHAPTER 5: HORTICULTURAL THERAPY

1. Paul Mills, "VA's Flower Therapy," *V.F.W. Magazine* 63 (November 1975): 36–37.

2. Gene Rothert, *The Enabling Garden* (Dallas: Taylor Publishing, 1994).

3. Bibby Moore, *Growing with Gardening: A Twelve-Month Guide for Therapy, Recreation and Education* (Chapel Hill: University of North Carolina Press, 1989).

4. Benjamin Rush, *Medical Inquiries and Observations upon Diseases of the Mind* (Philadelphia: Kimber and Richardson, 1812), 226.

5. E. R. Johnson, "The Value of Sense Training in Nature Study," *Journal of Psycho-Aesthenics* 4, no. 1 (1899): 213–17.

6. G. M. Lawrence, "Principle of Education for the Feeble Minded," *Journal of Psycho-Aesthenics* 4, no. 3 (1900): 100–108.

7. Helen Campbell, T. W. Knox, and T. Byrnes, *Darkness and Daylight; or, Lights and Shadows of New York Life* (Hartford: Hartford Publishing, 1896), 307, 309. Excerpted in National Council for Therapy and Rehabilitation through Horticulture, *Lecture and Publication Series* 1 (April 1975): 1–3.

8. Donald P. Watson and Alice W. Burlingame, *Therapy through Horticulture* (New York: Macmillan, 1960).

9. Eugene A. Rothert and James R. Daubert, *Horticultural Therapy at Physical Rehabilitation Facility* (Glencoe: Chicago Horticultural Society, 1981), 7.

10. Joan Bardach, "Some Principles of Horticultural Therapy with the Physically Disabled." Presented at the National Council for Therapy and Rehabilitation through Horticulture, Michigan State University, East Lansing, September 1975.

11. Swee-Lian Yi, "A Life Renewed," *National Gardening* 8 (September 1985): 19–21.

12. Swee-Lian Yi, "Gardening at the Guild for Exceptional Children," *NCTRH Newsletter* 13 (March 1986): 3.

13. Howard Brooks and C. D. Oppenheim, *Horticulture as a Therapeutic Aid,* monograph no. 49 (New York: New York University Medical Center Institute of Rehabilitation Medicine, 1973), 30.

14. Andrew L. Barber, "Horticultural Therapy," unpublished paper, Menninger Clinic, Topeka, Kansas, 3.

15. Ira Stamm and Andrew Barber, "The Nature of Change in Horticultural Therapy." Presented at the National Council for Therapy and Rehabilitation through Horticulture, Topeka, Kansas, September 1978, 12.

16. Stamm and Barber, "The Nature of Change," 13.

17. Ibid., 15.

18. Martha Strauss, interview with author, July 28, 1991.

19. Jay Stone Rice, "Self-Development and Horticultural Therapy in a Jail Setting," Ph.D. diss., Professional School of Psychology, San Francisco, 1993.

20. Ray Coleman, "Defining the Client: Who Are the Incarcerated?" *Proceedings,* Horticultural Therapy in Corrections Conference, Great Plains Chapter, National Council for Therapy and Rehabilitation through Horticulture, Kansas City, Missouri, 1982, 5.

21. Robert Neese, "Prisoner's Escape," *Flower Grower* 46, no. 8 (1959): 40.

22. Warren H. Adams, Jr., "A Personal Statement on Horticultural Therapy," National Council for Therapy and Rehabilitation through Horticulture *Newsletter* 6 (July 1979): 3.

23. Jeffery T. Philpott to author, September 13, 1991.

24. Quoted from Bob Conover with Pam Price, "The Lessons of Gardening," *San Francisco Urban Gardener* 7 (Summer 1989): 9, 12, 14.

Chapter 6: The Restorative Environment

1. Marcia June West, "Landscape Views and Stress Response in the Prison Environment," M.A. thesis, University of Washington, 1986, 5.

2. Andrew L. Turner, "The Therapeutic Value of Nature," *Journal of Operational Psychiatry* 6, no. 1 (1976): 64–74.

3. Turner, "The Therapeutic Value of Nature," 65.

4. Stephen Kaplan and Janet Frey Talbot, "Psychological Benefits of a Wilderness Experience," in *Behavior and the Natural Environment,* vol. 6 of *Human Behavior and Environment,* ed. Irwin Altman and Joachim E. Wohlwill (New York: Plenum, 1983), 163–203.

5. Kaplan and Talbot, "Psychological Benefits," 12.

6. Ibid., 179, 181.

7. Kaplan and Kaplan, *The Experience of Nature.*

8. Ibid., 185.

9. Roger S. Ulrich, "View through a Window May Influence Recovery from Surgery," *Science* 224 (1984): 420–21.

10. Ernest O. Moore, "A Prison Environment's Effect on Health Care Service Demands," *Journal of Environmental Systems* 11, no. 1 (1981–82): 17–33; West, "Landscape Views and Stress."

11. West, "Landscape Views and Stress," 94.

12. Judith H. Heerwegen and Gordon H. Orians, "Adaptation to Windowlessness: A Study of the Use of Visual Decor in Windowed and Windowless Offices," *Environment and Behavior* 18 (September 1986): 623–39.

13. James A. Wise and Erika Rosenberg, *The Effects of Interior Treatments on Performance Stress in Three Types of Mental Tasks,* Technical Report 002-02-1988 (Allendale, Mich.: Center for Integrated Facilities Research, F. E. Seidman School of Business, 1988).

14. Ulrich et al., "Stress Recovery during Exposure to Natural and Urban Environments," 208.

15. Stainbrook, "Man's Psychic Needs for Nature," 22.

CHAPTER 7: TOWARD A GREEN TOMORROW

1. Andrew C. Hiatt, *Production of Monoclonal Antibody in Plants* (La Jolla: Research Institute of Scripps Clinic, 1989).

2. Robert Lee Holtz, "Vaccines in Your Vegetables," *Los Angeles Times,* November 23, 1993, A1, A3.

3. Gert Groening and Joachim Wolsche-Buhlman, "Some Notes on the Mania for Native Plants in Germany," *Landscape Journal* 11 (Fall 1992): 116–26; Gert Groening and Joachim Wolsche-Bulman, "Politics, Planning and the Protection of Nature: Political Abuse of Early Ecological Ideas in Germany, 1933–45," *Planning Perspectives* 2 (1987): 127–48.

4. Groening and Wolsche-Bulman, "Politics, Planning," 138.

5. Groening and Wolsche-Bulman, "Some Notes," 122

6. D. F. Karnosky and S. L. Karnosky, eds., *Improving the Quality of Urban Life with Plants,* publication no. 2 (New York: New York Botanical Garden, 1985); Mark Francis and Randy Hester, eds., *Proceedings: Meanings of the Garden* (Davis: Center for Design Research, University of California, Davis, 1987).

7. Diane Relf, ed., *The Role of Horticulture in Human Well-Being and Social Development* (Portland: Timber Press, 1992).

8. Steven Kaplan to the author, February 12, 1994.

CONCLUSION

1. Joseph W. Meeker, *Minding the Earth* (Alameda, Calif.: Latham Foundation, 1988), 31.

2. James Swan, *Sacred Places* (Santa Fe: Bear, 1990), 137.

3. McHarg, *Design with Nature,* 28.

4. Suzanne Fields, "Bennett Book Quantifies Cultural Decline," *Albuquerque Journal,* 1994, A14.

5. Edward O. Wilson, *Biophilia* (Cambridge: Harvard University Press, 1984).

6. David W. Orr, "Love It or Lose It: The Coming Biophilia Revolution," in *The Biophihlia Hypothesis,* ed. S. R. Kellert and E. O. Wilson (Washington: Island Press, 1993), 437.

7. Jim Lollman, *Why We Garden* (New York: Henry Holt, 1994), 102.

8. Lollman, *Why We Garden,* 103.

9. Michael Pollan, *Second Nature* (New York: Atlantic Monthly Press, 1991), 190–96.

Index

Page numbers in *italics* refer to illustrations.

Acacia tortilis, 19, *20,* 21
Adolescents. *See* Children and adolescents
Ailanthus altissima, 26
Anaya, Bodil Dresher, 84–85
Animals, 23, 80
Appleton, Jay, 16
Appraised threat in settings, defined, 16
Arbor Day, 66
Are, Jean, 92
Atmosphere of earth, impact of green nature
    on, 5–6, 12, 67, 72

Balling, John D., 20
Barber, Andrew, 94–95
Bardach, Joan, 81
Barred, Nancy, 114
Beverly Farm Foundation (Godfrey, Ill.), 86
Biomes, defined, 19
Biophilia, defined, 130
Bloedel, Prentice, 36
Bloedel Reserve (Wash.), 31, 35–38
Bloedel, Virginia, 36
Body wisdom, accumulation of, 10–12, 13, 17–
    19, 76
Brooks, Howard, 83
Brown, Lancelot (Capability), 28
Buildings, integration of plants and, 30–31,
    113–14

Burlingame, Alice, *Therapy through
    Horticulture,* 79
Bush-Brown, Louise, 58, 59, 73

Campbell, Helen, 77
Charles II (king of Great Britain), 27
Chejfec, Gregorio, 113–14
Children and adolescents, 57; horticulture
    therapy for, 78, 86, 87, 96–97, 100;
    intergenerational gardening with, 91–94, 98;
    landscape preferences by, 20–21;
    participation in urban greening by, 69–71;
    wilderness experiences for, 107–10
Chi as unified creation (China), 132
Church, Thomas, 37
Cities. *See* Urban settings
Coherence of landscapes, defined, 14
Coleman, Ray, 99–100
Combustion and greenhouse effect, 5
Community, sense of: from urban forestry
    projects, 67–73; from urban gardening
    projects, 54–62, 63, 65, 72–73
Complexity of landscapes, defined, 14
Complexity in settings, defined, 16
Copus, Earl, 79
Correctional institutions: horticulture therapy
    in, 99–103; restorative nature of views from
    windows in, 112–13
Cousineau, Christine, 54
Cousino, Ida, 97, 98

Cultures and influences: and commonalities in landscape preferences, 13–14, 16, 17, 19; in responses to green nature, 26–28, 56, 57; on use of versus experience of nature, 8–9, 130–31

Daubert, James R., 80
Davis, Stephen, 79
Deflected vista in settings, defined, 16
Depth in settings, defined, 16
Design with Nature (McHarg), 9
Developmental disabilities, horticulture therapy for, 75, *75*, 85–87
Dillard, Annie, 23
DuBos, René, 8
Dumont, Matthew, 65

Eastern cultures, 132
Elderly. *See* Geriatric centers
Emotional responses to nature, 23, 51–52; as noncognitive, 18, 44–48. *See also* Horticulture therapy; Innate responses
England, garden styles of, 27–28
Epstein, Sandra, 93, 94
Everden, Neil, 47
Evolution: and body wisdom accumulation in humans, 10–12, 13, 17–19; and genetic memory, 19, 21, 107; and interpretation of environmental clues for survival, 13–24; and restorative qualities of green nature, 115, 116–17; and rhythms in gardening, 4, 63, 65; as thirty-minute film, 12, 133. *See also* Humans, primitive
Experience of Place (Hiss), 47

Falk, John H., 20
Felt sense, 44–47; defined, 46
Focality in settings, 37; defined, 14–16
Forestry in urban settings, 65–73
France, garden style in, 27
Frazel, Matthew, 86

Gardening, 133; adaptive, *75*, 76, *89*, 90; as evaluation tool, 76, 84, 96; and history of garden styles, 21, 27–28; as horticulture therapy, 74–105; for peace of mind, 53–54, 65, 73, 100, 105, 118; in physical and mental gardens, 50–52; process of, 8, 51–53, 61, 73, 105; reasons for effectiveness of, 63–65; self-esteem growth through, 54–58, 63, 73, 99–

100, 102; as *tikkun olam*, 61–62; urban and community forestry as, 65–73. *See also* Gardening projects and programs; Landscapes

Gardening organizations: American Association of Botanical Gardens and Arboreta, 127; American Community Gardening Association, 65; American Forestry Association, 71; American Horticultural Society, 53; American Society for Horticultural Science, 127; International Society for Horticultural Science, 127; National Aborist Association, 71–72; National Council of State Garden Clubs, 78; Neighborhood Gardening Association, 58; Pennsylvania Horticultural Society, 59; U.S. Department of Agriculture, 66; U.S. Forest Service, 66, 71. *See also* Gardening projects and programs; Volunteer groups

Gardening projects and programs: Columbus Garden project, 60; ICA Fifth City gardening, 60–61; Joel Schnaper Memorial Garden, 62; Minnesota Green programs, 59–60; Neighborhood Gardening Association window-box program, 58–59; Neighborwoods Program, 65–66; NYCHA garden contest, 54–58; Open Lands Project, 65–66, 69; Philadelphia Green programs, 59; P-Patch Community Gardening Program, 62; Robert M. Kubecka Memorial Organic Garden, 62; Urban and Community Forestry Program, 66. *See also* Gardening; Gardening organizations; Volunteer groups

Gedlin, Eugene, 46
Genetic engineering, 122–24
Geriatric centers, horticulture therapy in, 88–94
Global warming, 5–6
Greenhouse effect, 5–6
Green nature: adaptability of, 1–3, 119; biocentric view of, 131–34; as biologically similar to humans, 4, 119, 134; cultural influences on reactions to, 8–9, 26–28, 56, 57, 130–31; evolution as influence on reactions to, 10–24; as experience, 44–48; future of, 121–34; gardening as participation with, 49–73; and history of vegetation in urban settings, 28–31; and horticulture therapy, 94–98; identification of, 6–8; as resource to be used, 47–48, 129–34; as

restorative environment, 29, 106–20; in role of sustaining human life, 3–6; and settings designed to influence emotions, 31–43
Groening, Gert, 124–25
Ground texture in settings, defined, 16
Gutowski, Robert, 66–67

Haag, Richard, 37
Hamilton, Arlene, 101–2
Healing through gardening, 61–62, 73. *See also* Horticulture therapy
Heerwagen, Judith, 19, 21
Hein, Mich B., 123
Hester, Randy, 126
Hiatt, Andrew C., 122–23
High-density areas. *See* Urban settings
Himmler, Heinrich, 124–25
Hiss, Tony, 32; *Experience of Place,* 47
Hoerr, Suzanne, 65–66, 69
Hollister, Robert M., 54
Horticulture therapy: academic views on, 125–26; in correctional institutions, 99–103; for developmental disabilities, *75,* 76, 85–87; in geriatric centers, 88–94; in physical rehabilitation centers, 80–85; principles and history of, 62, 74–80, 86, 95, 99; in psychiatric centers, 94–98; qualities of plants for, 81–83, 89–90, 94–96, 103–5
Horticulture therapy organizations: American Horticultural Therapy Association, 79; Association for Retarded Citizens of New Mexico, 87; Brattleboro Retreat, 96–97; Chicago Botanic Garden, 75, 86, 94; Friends Asylum for the Insane, 77; Melwood Horticultural Training Center, 87; Menninger Foundation, 78–79; National Council for Therapy and Rehabilitation, 79; New York Horticultural Society (NYHS), 102–3; Rusk Institute, 81–84; Veterans Administration Medical Center, 97–98
Horticulture therapy projects and programs: in Breman Home for the Aged, 92–94; at East Side Lodging for Boys, 77; Enabling Garden for People with Disabilities, 75, *75,* 89; "Glass Garden," 81–82; Master Gardener Program, 103; NYHS "Project Greenworks," 102–3; Vets Garden, 97–98
Human beings: as biologically similar to plants, 4, 119, 134; and body wisdom,

accumulation of, 10–12, 18–19; gardening and needs of, 64–65; identification of green nature by, 6–8; interpretation of nature's clues by, 22–24; intuitions of, 10–11, 16, 17, 95; landscape preferences by, 13–17, *15,* 19–22; on nature as resource to be used, 8–9, 47–48, 129–34; plants as necessary to life of, 4–6; survival of, with biocentric view of nature, 129–34. *See also* Human beings, primitive
Human beings, primitive: body wisdom, accumulation of, 10–12, 13, 17–19, 76; interpretation of environmental clues by, 17–24; landscape preferences of, 13, 16–17, 19–20, 21; modern society out of sync with, 4, 117, 130, 131; and restorative qualities of green nature, 116–17. *See also* Evolution; Human beings
Hypnotherapy, 108

ICA (Institute of Cultural Affairs), 60–61
Innate responses: "fight or flee" response, 11; as genetic memory, 19, 21, 107; in landscape preference, 13–19, 21–22; transgenerational transmission of, 17, 19, 21. *See also* Emotional responses
Institute of Cultural Affairs (ICA), 60–61
Intuition. *See* Innate responses
Italy, landscape style of, 28

Japan, landscape and garden styles of, 21–22, 37, 56
Johnson, Lyndon B., 54
Jordan, Mark B., 100–101

Kamp, David, 62
Kaplan, Maxine, 88
Kaplan, Rachel: on decoding landscapes, 14; on micro-restorative environments, 111; on significance of gardening, 53–54, 65; on wilderness experiences, 108, 109, 110
Kaplan, Stephen, 127; on decoding landscapes, 14; on micro-restorative environments, 111; on significance of gardening, 53–54; on wilderness experiences, 108, 109, 110
Korea, landscape design in, 26

Landscapes, 114; of Bloedel Reserve, 36–38; geometric designs in history of, 27–28; of Morton Arboretum, 32–33, 34–35; noncognitive perception of, 45–46;

preferences for, 13–17, *15*, 19–22; qualities used in decoding of, 14; of savannas, 19–22; social and political manipulation of, 124–25; variables affecting information from, 14–17. *See also* Gardening

Lanphear, Lauren, 72

La Paloma Greenhouses (Corrales, N.M.), 87

Lawrence, G. M., 77

Leakey, Richard, 21

Learey, Fred, 68

Learning, 18, 73, 109–10. *See also* Gardening projects and programs; Horticulture therapy projects and programs

Legibility of landscapes, defined, 14

Le Notre, Andre, 27

Leopold, Aldo, *Sand County Almanac*, 9

Link, Conrad, 79

Lipkis, Andy, 65

Lipkis, Katie, 65

Louis XIV (king of France), 27

Mattson, Richard, 79

McCandliss, Rhea, 78, 79

McCurdy, Eleanor, 79

McHarg, Ian, 129; *Design with Nature*, 9

Medical science, future of green nature in, 121–24

Melwood Horticultural Training Center (Upper Marlboro, Md.), 87

Menninger, F. C., 78

Menninger, Karl, 78, 79

Mental disabilities. *See* Developmental disabilities

Mental fatigue, 117–18

Mental gardens, 50–52, 114

Meyers, Sid, 96–97

Micro-restorative environments, 111, 120

Mills, Paul, 74

Morris Arboretum (Pa.), Center for Urban Forestry, 66–67

Morton Arboretum (Ill.), 26, 31–35, *35*

Morton, Joy, 31

Morton, Julius Sterling, 66

Mystery of landscapes, defined, 14

Native Americans, 76, 91; on interconnectedness of all life, 106, 132, 134

Netherlands, landscape design in, 26

New York City Housing Authority (NYCHA) garden contest, 54–58

Noncognitive experiences, 18, 44–48. *See also* Emotional responses

NYCHA. *See* New York City Housing Authority (NYCHA) garden contest

O'Donoghue, Tom, 113–14

Olmsted, Frederick Law, 6–7, 28–29

Organic Gardening and Farming magazine, 53–54

Orians, Gordon, 19, 21

Orr, David W., 130

Paley Park (N.Y.), 29–30

Parks: and forests in urban settings, 65–73; historical overview of, in United States, 28–29; as "lungs" for cities, 28–30; as restorative environments, 3, 6–7, 106; in urban settings, 20, 26, 29–43

Peace of mind, 44, 84, 94–95; Bloedel Reserve design for, 35–38; from gardening, 53–54, 65, 73, 100, 105, 118; at Morton Arboretum, 31; in Vets Garden, 97–98; from wilderness experiences, 109–10. *See also* Restorative environment

People-Plant Council, 127

People-plant relationship: biological link, 4, 119, 134; Bloedel Reserve design for, 35, 38; in future of horticulture, 125–27; through horticulture therapy, 74–105; interconnectedness in, 8, 52–53, 56, 63, 104–5, 131

Perception, simultaneous, 47; defined, 32

Philpott, Jeffrey T., 101

Photosynthesis, 4–6

Physical rehabilitation centers, horticulture therapy at, 80–85

Politics and future of green nature, 124–25

Pollan, Michael, 133

Preference, theory of, 16. *See also* Landscapes, preferences for

Prisons. *See* Correctional institutions

Prospect of settings, *15*; defined, 16

Protection. *See* Survival

Psychiatric centers, horticulture therapy in, 94–98

Refuges: Bloedel Reserve (Wash.), 31, 35–38; Morton Arboretum (Ill.), 26, 31–35, *35*; Walt Disney World (Fla.), 31, 40–43, *41*. *See also* Parks

Refuge of settings, *15*; defined, 16

Relf, Diane Hefley, 79, 126, 127
Religion. *See* Spirituality
Repton, Humphrey, 28
Restorative environment: measurement of, 115–16; Morton Arboretum design for, 34–35; need for, 106–7; qualities of, 29, 34–35, 110, 116–20; and substitutes for wilderness experiences, 111–14; wilderness experiences as, 107–11. *See also* Peace of mind; Stress reduction
Rothert, Eugene A., 80
Rush, Benjamin, 77
Ruth Taylor Geriatric Center (Valhalla, N.Y.), 88

Safety. *See* Survival
Sand County Almanac (Leopold), 9
Savannas: defined, 19; landscape preference for, 19–22
Schroeder, Herbert W., 34, 46
Seasons, changes in, 22–23, 51
Self-esteem: of dysfunctional persons, 82, 96; in urban settings, 54, 63
Self-esteem, growth of, 87; through gardening, 54–58, 63, 73, 99–100, 102; in wilderness experiences, 109–10
Senses: function of, 7, 18, 62; identification of setting by, 6–8, 25–26
Sheppard, Paul, 47
Sheppard-Pratt Hospital (Baltimore), 96
Sigler, Maurice, 100
Simultaneous perception, 47; defined, 32
Smith, Mark, 86
Snead, Cathy, 101–2
Society, 132; ever-increasing stress in, 47, 106, 130; on nature as resource to be used, 8–9, 47–48, 129
Spirituality: God-centered view of life, 61, 130; in green nature experiences, 34–35, 37, 110
Stainbrook, Edward, 63, 117
Stieber, Nancy, 45, 46
Strauss, Martha, 96
Stress reduction, 11; horticulture therapy for, 85, 96; and measurement of stress, 14, 115–16; through micro-restorative environments, 111–13, 114, 120; Morton Arboretum design for, 31–36, 35; and stress as ever-increasing today, 47, 106, 117, 130; in urban settings, 3, 12, 31, 67. *See also* Peace of mind; Restorative environment

Sunlight, 5–6
Survival: with biocentric view of nature, 129–34; interpretation of landscape clues for, 13, 16–22; interpretation of nature's signs for, 22–24; safety and protection for, 15, 16, 17–18, 19. *See also* Stress reduction

Talbot, Janet Fry, 108, 109, 110
Taylor, Sid, 87
Technology, 8, 64–65, 114
Therapy through Horticulture (Watson and Burlingame), 79
Thoreau, Henry David, 9
Tikkun olam, gardening as, 61–62
Training programs: and horticulture therapy as training, 74–105; at Melwood Horticultural Training Center, 87; Outward Bound as, 107; on people-plant relationships, 126–27; on tree care for volunteers, 68–69; vocational training in horticulture, 87, 96, 99, 100–101
Turner, Andrew L., 108

Ulrich, Roger S.: on effects of nature scenes, 111–12, 115–16, 119; on informational qualities of landscapes, 14–16
United States: "America the Beautiful" bill (1991), 66; Cooperative Forestry Assistance Act (1978), 66; Department of Agriculture, 66; Forest Service, 66, 71; green movements in, 124, 125; historical overview of parks in, 26, 28–29; symptoms of dysfunction in, 91, 130
Urban settings: benefits of green nature in, 28–31, 75; forestry in, 65–73; history of, 2–3, 116–17; parks and greenery in, 29–43; and physical condition as influence on self-esteem, 54, 63; in research on landscape preferences, 13–14; sensual identification of, 25–26; stress reduction in, 3, 12, 31, 67. *See also* Gardening projects and programs; Volunteer groups

V.F.W. Magazine, 74
Vocational training. *See* Training programs
Volunteer groups: awards for, 71; Citizen Foresters, 69; Citizen Pruner Tree Care Program, 69; Friends of the Urban Forest, 67, 68; Global ReLEAF, 71; Green Guerrillas, 67; Kids for a Clean Environment (KIDS

FACE), 71; Master Tree Steward Program, 69; People for Trees, 68; Releaf Anaheim, 67; Re-Tree Schenectady, 67; training for, 68–69; Treekeepers, 65–66, 69; Tree Musketeers, 67, 70–71; TreePeople, 65; Trees Atlanta, 67; Twin Cities Tree Trust, 67. *See also* Gardening organizations; Gardening projects and programs

Wagner, Richard H., 12
Walt Disney World (Fla.), 31, 40–43, *41*
Ward, Barbara, 8
Warner, Katy Moss, 42, 43
Watson, Donald P., *Therapy through Horticulture,* 79

Weather changes, 22–23
Well-being. *See* Peace of mind
West, Marcia June, 113
Western society. *See* Society
Whitlesey, Lisa, 103
Wilderness experiences: as restorative environment, 107–11; restorative substitutes for, 111–14
William Breman Jewish Home for the Aged (Atlanta), 92–93
Wilson, Edward O., 130
Wolsche-Bulmahn, Joachim, 124–25
Wordsworth, William, "The Rainbow," 6, 24

Yi, Swee-Lian, 82–83

CHARLES A. LEWIS attended the University of Maryland and Cornell University and has worked as a plant breeder, garden center operator, and then director of Sterling Forest Gardens in Tuxedo, New York. He has also been horticulturist, administrator of collections, and research fellow at the Morton Arboretum in Lisle, Illinois. His work has been honored by the American Horticultural Society, American Horticultural Therapy Association, U.S. Department of Argriculture, Swarthmore College, New York City Housing Authority, and the Chicago Housing Authority. He lives in Albuquerque, New Mexico.

UNIVERSITY OF ILLINOIS PRESS
1325 SOUTH OAK STREET
CHAMPAIGN, ILLINOIS 61820-6903
WWW.PRESS.UILLINOIS.EDU